The Gift of Sexuality:
Empowerment for Religious Teens

Steve Clapp

A LifeQuest Publication

The Gift of Sexuality
Empowerment for Religious Teens

Steve Clapp

For further information, contact: LifeQuest, 6404 S. Calhoun Street, Fort Wayne, Indiana 46807; DadofTia@aol.com; 260-744-5010.

The author of this book is not a medical professional. While every attempt has been made to ensure the accuracy of information about topics such as contraception, HIV/AIDS, and other sexually transmitted diseases, you should always depend on a physician for counsel on medical matters.

The names and/or locations of some persons quoted in this book have been changed to protect their privacy.

Biblical quotations, except for Chapter Nine, are from the New Revised Standard Version of the Bible, copyrighted 1989 by the Division of Christian Education, National Council of Churches and are used by permission. The Chapter Nine quotes are from the Today's English Version, copyrighted 1976 by the American Bible Society and are used by permission.

ISBN 1–893270–32–7

Library of Congress Control Number 2005936466

Manufactured in the United States of America

Contents

**This book is dedicated
to teenagers across the United States
who want to relate their faith
to their sexual decisions
and
to the clergy, youth workers,
and parents
who are seeking to help them.**

I feel a significant debt to many people who influenced the **Faith Matters** *project on which this book is based. I received especially significant guidance along the way from Jeremy Ashworth, Doug Bauder, Debra W. Haffner, and Martin Siegel. I have also been influenced by the work of others in related fields including Douglas Kirby, Diane di Mauro, and James Nelson.*

This book has been significantly influenced by the persons mentioned above and also by Marcia Egbert, Jan Fairchild, Dr. Dean Frank, Ann Hanson, Kristen Leverton Helbert, Jerry Peterson, Stacey Sellers, Holly Sprunger, Sara Sprunger, and Angela Zizak. The teens and adults who helped in the field testing process have significantly improved the quality of this book. My earlier collaboration with Julie Seibert Berman and Sue Brownfield continues to influence my work with teens.

The George Gund Foundation provided the primary funding for the development of this resource. Christian Community's work in the area of youth and sexuality has been helped by these foundations: The Compton Foundation, The Lutheran Foundation, and The Charles Stewart Mott Foundation. Related work has been helped by the Ford Foundation, the William and Flora Hewlett Foundation, the W.T. Grant Foundation, and the Robert Sterling Clark Foundation.

So now, O Israel, what does the LORD your God require of you? Only to fear the LORD your God, to walk in all his ways, to love him, to serve the LORD your God with all your heart and with all your soul, and to keep the commandments of the LORD your God and his decrees that I am commanding you today, for your own well-being.
Deuteronomy 10:12–13

Just then a lawyer stood up to test Jesus. "Teacher," he said, "what must I do to inherit eternal life?" He said to him, "What is written in the law? What do you read there?" He answered, "You shall love the Lord your God with all your heart, and with all your soul, and with all your strength, and with all your mind; and your neighbor as yourself."
Luke 10:25–27

Chapter One
For Youth Only

When I got pregnant, my minister was so kind and helpful to me. I'll never forget how he got my parents to stop being angry. . . . But where was the church before I got pregnant? If I'd understood the way my faith should shape my decisions, I don't think I would have had intercourse. And why didn't the church or anyone else teach me about pills or condoms? I know what I did is my responsibility, but the right information could have changed my life.

Female Teenager

The teenager who shared those words is right. The minister came through for her in a time of tremendous need, but her congregation and other adults could have helped her avoid becoming pregnant in the first place. I've written this book to provide the information and guidance that religious young people need to make healthy decisions about sexual values and behaviors.

This book is for youth only. Well, sort of. Parents, clergy, and other concerned adults are welcome to read it and probably should read it, but they need to proceed with an awareness that the book is addressed to teenagers, not adults. My preparation for writing this book included directing a survey of almost 6,000 teenagers around the United States in which they were asked to share frankly about their religious faith, their congregational activity, their sexual values, and their sexual behaviors. The full results of that research are published in another book called *Faith Matters*. I'll share some of those results in this book. I've also visited with hundreds of young people to ask their guidance on the information they would like to have in a book written just for them.

Adults reading this book should fasten their seat belts. I'm providing the facts about what religious young people have and have not done sexually and about how they feel about those activities. I'm also providing readers the information about topics like oral sex, intercourse, contraception, abortion, HIV, other sexually transmitted diseases, and homosexuality that teens have told me they need. I'm doing so because the survey and my own work with teenagers over the years have convinced me that young people make responsible decisions when given accurate information.

While I certainly hope that this book will be read by some teenagers who are not connected with any religion, I am writing especially for young people who are involved in congregations and for whom their faith is important. In responses to the national survey, teens made it clear that they want to relate their belief in God to their decisions about dating, sexuality, marriage, and parenting. Too often, however, those of us who are adults have failed to provide the needed facts.

We live in a strange time in terms of sexuality. Sex pervades the media: television, motion pictures, the Internet, newspapers, magazines, and books. Advertisers frequently use implied or explicit sex to sell their products. Yet large numbers of adults are uncomfortable talking about sexuality with one another or with young people.

Teenagers have learned from adults to feel uncomfortable talking about sexuality. The young people who responded to the survey said that it is sometimes easier to just have sex than to talk about whether or not to have it. But the decision to have sexual intercourse, oral sex, or other intimate sexual activity is a life-transforming decision. We are not the same and the relationship is not the same after that kind of experience.

Talking about sexuality is really not that difficult—we just feel like it is. You might consider this book "talking about sexuality" from one caring adult to teenagers who read it. If your mother, father, minister, priest, rabbi, youth worker, or teacher has given the book to you, then it is likely that you can have a conversation with that person about the topics covered in these pages. I hope you will go to that person to talk more about these topics.

This book is about sex, but it is also about a lot more than sex. Our sexual values, decisions, and behaviors grow out of the kind of people we are; the kinds of relationships we have with others; and the kind of relationship we have with God. The teens who responded to the survey made it clear that they would like more help in thinking about not only sex but also dating, marriage, and parenting.

Sex can be pleasurable, good, downright fun. Many adults are terrified of saying that to teenagers. They are afraid that acknowledging how enjoyable sexual activities can be will cause teenagers to immediately go out and start doing those things. But the truth is that sex can be one of the most enjoyable aspects of life. For those of us in the Jewish and Christian traditions, our sexuality is a good gift from a loving God. It's part of the way we are made, and sex can be a wonderful activity for people who are committed to each other.

Unprotected sex, of course, can have many negative consequences. Unwanted pregnancies, abortions, HIV [the virus that causes AIDS], and other sexually transmitted diseases can all result from people participating in sexual activities without protection. Unwanted pregnancy can interrupt or even end a person's education. HIV literally kills. Too many young people are victims of sexual abuse, rape, and other unwanted activities.

Sex can have negative consequences for people even if nothing like rape or pregnancy or disease results from it. Sexual activities touch the very core of who we are as human beings. People experience great hurt when they share in sexual activities with a person who turns out not to respect them or not to feel the same way about the relationship or not to be committed to them.

Adults know those realities about sex. Some adults know the realities especially well because they have made mistakes about sexual decisions in their own lives. As a result, they become very nervous when talking about sex with teenagers. They don't want to be responsible for a young person making a serious mistake in judgment. But the failure of adults to talk about these things causes teenagers to have inadequate information for decision-making.

And while there are many factors to be considered before sharing in a sexual activity with another person, the fact remains that caring sexual behaviors with the right person can be fun. Sexual intercourse is also the means by which we share with God in creating new life. God made it that way.

What Do You Know?

As you start this book, it may be helpful to think about what you already know and do not know concerning some of the topics that will be covered. Mark an **X** on the line following each item to show how characteristic that item is of you. **7** indicates "very characteristic" and **1** indicates "not at all characteristic."

You may want to come back to this exercise again at the end of the book. If you do not feel, after reading the pages that follow, that you have gained in your understanding of an area, it is either because you already knew a great deal about it or because I didn't do a good job writing. I'll provide information on how to contact me at the end of the book.

1. I understand what all these words or phrases mean: erection, penis, testes, vagina, labia, clitoris, orgasm, masturbation, ejaculation, HIV, sexually transmitted diseases, oral sex, hymen, the pill, the patch, sexual intercourse.

7	6	5	4	3	2	1

2. I have a good understanding of what happens during male and female sexual response. I understand sexual arousal; why men often have orgasms before women; and what an orgasm is.

7	6	5	4	3	2	1

3. I can talk about sexuality comfortably with my parents and other significant adults in my life. If I have questions or face a sexual problem, I know there is an adult who will help me.

7	6	5	4	3	2	1

4. I can talk about sexuality comfortably with one or more friends. I do not feel embarrassed in talking about sexual concerns and can be honest about my own anxieties.

7	6	5	4	3	2	1

5. On a date, I can comfortably [or feel that I could comfortably] talk with the person I am dating about my own sexual desires and limits. I could listen to and respect the desires and limits of the other person.

7	6	5	4	3	2	1

6. I am always respectful of myself and of others as the children of God.

7	6	5	4	3	2	1

7. I understand what the Bible and my faith tradition say about sexuality, and I know how to relate my faith to sexual decisions.

7	6	5	4	3	2	1

8. I know what characteristics are important to me in a marriage partner. I have worked through in my own mind the difference between the characteristics which attract me to someone and the characteristics which I would value in a marriage.

7	6	5	4	3	2	1

9. I am aware of my own sexual orientation, and I understand at least some of the reasons why not all persons have a hetero-sexual orientation.

7	6	5	4	3	2	1

10. I am clear about my own values in the area of sexuality. I know under what circumstances and with what kind of person I am personally willing to share in sexual activities. I know the level of sexual activity that is right for me at this point in my life.

7	6	5	4	3	2	1

11. I understand the contributions to my sexual values which have been made by my parents, friends, school, congregation, the Bible, television, magazines, and the Internet. I know how to comfortably sort through conflicting information.

7	6	5	4	3	2	1

12. I have a good understanding of contraception and know how to protect myself and a partner against both pregnancy and sexually transmitted disease.

7	6	5	4	3	2	1

Chapter Two
For Adults Who Are Looking at This Book

*I'm threatened by the idea of a public school or a
parochial school being where my son and daughter
learn about sex. But I have to confess that I'm also
uncomfortable discussing these matters with my kids.
That makes me feel like a hypocrite. I know they talk
about sex with their friends, probably every day, and
I know they get all kinds of information from television and the Internet. It's time for parents and the
church to start helping teens, but we need a little
help in that process.*

American Baptist Parent

Adults from many denominational traditions can identify
with the Baptist parent of two teenagers who shared those
words. As parents, clergy, youth workers, and other adults who
care about teens, we are very concerned about where they
receive their information about sexuality; and we are also
concerned about the beliefs and values that are communicated
along with the information.

Many of us support sexuality education in the schools, so
that all young people receive at least some of the basic
information they need. But whether for or against sexuality
education in the schools, most of us feel that parents and
religious communities should be the primary providers of sexual
information and values to the young people we love. With sex
education nonexistent in many schools and with many of us
uncomfortable dealing with the topic in the home or the congregation, teenagers are left dependent on their friends, television,
the Internet, magazines, and other sources for this information.

Those concerns form a large part of the motivation for the
writing and production of the book you are holding in your
hands. The book was written for youth. This short chapter is
the only one addressed to adults. But the book is intended as a
resource or a tool that caring adults can use to help young
people have the information that they need.

An *Adult Guide* is available as a companion to this book. You may well want to obtain a copy of the *Guide* to help you in working with young people who are reading this book or participating in a study based on it.

The Gift of Sexuality can be used in three primary ways:

1. This book can be given directly to teenagers for personal reading. The book has been written to be understandable and interesting to teens who read it without any further adult guidance. I have worked hard to be faithful to Scripture and to the major faith traditions in the pages that follow. I hope that adults will be comfortable letting teens have direct access to the book.

2. Some parents may want to give this book to their teenagers as a basis for dialogue with them. The *Adult Guide* gives suggestions for that kind of approach.

3. The book can be used as the basis for small group, Sunday school class, fellowship group, or retreat study. The *Adult Guide* contains suggested activities and discussion guidelines for those who would like to use the book in that way.

It's important for adults looking at the book to understand seven important assumptions that provide the grounding for the pages that follow:

One, I am convinced that both adults and teenagers need access to information about what teenage sexual practices actually are and how teens feel about the sexual experiences they have had. Those of us who are adults need that information to jar us out of the complacency with which we have attempted to ignore this area of teen life.

Teenagers need access to information on sexual behavior for two reasons. First, without such information, it is too easy to assume that other teens are more sexually active than they in fact are. The *Faith Matters* study, described more fully in the Appendix, sought information from almost 6,000 religious teens. The data from that study shows that the range of expected sexual behavior for teens is very broad. While many are engaging in sexual intercourse and oral sex, the majority of religious teenagers are not doing so.

No one should be pushed into premature sexual activity on the basis that "everyone does it." Adults seeing the survey data for the first time tend to react with shock at how many teens have participated in oral sex and sexual intercourse. Many teens, however, are surprised that the percentages are not higher than they are. Knowing what others are actually doing helps one put in perspective what immediate peers claim "everyone" does. Knowing the mixed feelings that many teens have about early sexual activity can help other teens think more carefully about such decisions.

Second, many teenagers, like adults, find it far easier to talk about sexual behavior and values in terms of the survey results than in terms of their own experiences. In the area of sexuality, I can talk about what *others* do and believe more safely than about what I personally do and believe. As I have had opportunity to share the data from the *Faith Matters* study with youth groups, I have repeatedly found them willing to discuss the survey and the issues raised by the survey.

Two, teenagers have a right to direct access to good sexual information. When young people do not receive the information that they need, early sexual activity, teen pregnancy, abortion, HIV/AIDS, other sexually transmitted diseases, rape, and sexual abuse can all be a result. Young people pay a price when those of us in the religious community fail to take seriously our responsibility to them.

I am personally convinced that the majority of teenagers make responsible decisions when they are provided with accurate information. Both secular studies and the *Faith Matters* study confirm that teaching young people about contraception and about sexually transmitted diseases does not make them more likely to engage in early sexual activity. In the *Faith Matters* study, eight percent of responding congregations provided information about contraception. Those congregations reported no instances of pregnancy. Youth from those congregations were not any more likely or less likely than other youth in the study to have had sexual intercourse. The provision of the information does not make them more likely to be sexually active but does give them protection if they are.

Three, teenagers who embrace the Christian or Jewish faith will make sexual decisions in a religious framework if supported by caring adults. Because decisions about dating, marriage, sexual activity, and parenting are moral and spiritual decisions; parents and religious institutions are the ones with the responsibility for imparting the beliefs, values, and information to shape those decisions. While there are important reasons for having sexuality education available through the public schools, it is not the job of public schools to impart the spiritual foundation that those of us in the religious community can offer young people in their decision-making.

Four, the Bible does not support the repressive view of sexuality which too many of us in congregations have attempted to impose on teenagers. Too many of us in the church and synagogue have been too quick to focus on a small number of biblical passages that are prohibitive in nature. We have not wanted to call attention to the kind of celebration of love and sexuality found throughout the Hebrew Bible and New Testament in such books as the Song of Solomon. We have also not helped teens understand the implications of teachings of love, grace, and forgiveness for the intimate relationships that they have with others.

When teens find the repressive view of sexuality that is so often presented by congregations in conflict with their own experiences and desires, increasing numbers reject the congregation's influence in this area of life. This may also cause them to reject the faith in other areas. Those of us who are adults need to help teens see that decisions about dating, sex, marriage, and parenting are, at the core, spiritual decisions.

Five, evidence exists from secular studies that short-term efforts at sexuality education are helpful but that many other factors are involved in helping lower early sexual activity by teens. How young people feel about themselves, how successful they are in school, and how connected they are with their family and significant adults can all have an impact on how early they commence sexual activity. In *No Easy Answers*, an excellent publication from the National Campaign to Prevent Teen Pregnancy, Douglas Kirby writes that for more impact, programs "need to effectively address a greater number of risk and protective factors over a long period of time" [p. 1].

Because congregations relate to children and their parents from the time of birth, there are numerous opportunities to help guide the development of young people in positive ways:

16

- Service projects and other experiences that help build the self-esteem of youth are a routine part of the life of many congregations.

- Worship and religious education help shape the spiritual lives and moral decision-making ability of youth.

- Relationships with clergy, teachers, youth workers, and other religious mentors can have tremendous influence on the self-esteem and the values of youth.

If age-appropriate sexuality education is added to the many other positive experiences congregations make possible for youth, the potential exists for significant impact on their lives. Congregations are in fact ideal settings for sexuality education.

Six, the teachings of the Christian, Jewish, Muslim, Hindu, and Buddhist traditions include an emphasis on reaching out to people who are in need. The values of compassion, generosity, hospitality, and concern about justice are common to all the major faith traditions. Teen pregnancy, HIV/AIDS, and poverty are realities which people of faith would like to reduce. Churches and other faith-based institutions can help not only their own young people but also young people in the community. With congregations in every neighborhood in the United States, there is tremendous potential for positive impact on these social problems if faith-based institutions can identify effective strategies. I hope this book can be a resource that will help churches in that process. Because it can stand alone without the necessity of being used in a class or group, teens can be encouraged to give copies of this to their friends.

Seven, young people need information and guidance to help them prepare for dating, marriage, and parenting. While it is very important to provide young people with the factual information, the values, and the decision-making skills needed for healthy sexual choices, they need far more than that. Sexual decisions come within the context of dating, which leads in turn to marriage and parenting.

The *Faith Matters* study found that most congregations do not do much better helping teens prepare for dating, marriage, and parenting than helping them prepare for sexual decision-making. While the institution of marriage is certainly going through transitions, it remains one of the fundamental social institutions of our society. Yet we do very little to prepare young people for marriage. In the *Faith Matters* study, we found that clergy may offer marriage counseling after couples are engaged and that some congregations offer marriage preparation retreats for couples. Those efforts, however, come after people have made the decision about who their marriage partner will be. Young people need and want help understanding the nature of marriage and understanding the difference between factors that cause initial attraction and factors that result in lasting relationships.

Parenting may be the single most important job that many of us ever have. Yet our society as a whole does very little to prepare us to be good parents. Young people who fully understand the challenges of being a good parent are far less interested in taking on that role at an early age. Congregations have wonderful opportunities to help young people in this area.

Thus this book seeks to help young people not only with information, values, and skills for sexual decision-making but also with preparation for dating, marriage, and parenting.

Chapter Three
What Is Sexuality?

*People talk about sex like all it has to do with is
intercourse, but it feels like a whole lot more than
that to me. I'm aware of male–female differences
all the time. I relate to my mother differently than
my father. I'm not the same with my sister as I
am with my brother. I feel different with girls who
are friends than with guys who are friends, even
when the girls are people I don't want to date.*

Male Teenager

When many of us hear the word sexuality, our minds go to
those parts of the body known as genitals and to the activities
people do using those body parts. Most of us know that
sexuality is more than that, but we don't often think about what
the word means.

There are many definitions of sexuality, but I especially like
one shared by James B. Nelson: ***Sexuality is our way of being
in the world as male and female*** [From the book *Between
Two Gardens*, p. 5]. The Christian and Jewish traditions teach
that sexuality is a good gift from a loving God.

Our sexuality is both biological [as determined by our
chromosomes and our genitals] and culturally determined [how
we understand ourselves as masculine, feminine, or in-
between]. Our biological identity as sexual persons begins,
technically, at the moment of conception when sperm and egg
unite to form a male or a female embryo. From this moment on,
a person develops sexually and is influenced by different
experiences and people. Our gender identity is influenced as
soon as people in the delivery room ask about the newborn: is it
a boy or a girl?

While sexuality is not the whole of who we are, it is an
important component of who we are. As the male teenager
quoted at the start of this chapter says, there are gender
differences around us all the time. That doesn't mean that

males or females are superior or better–just that there are differences both in our bodies and in other ways as well.

The Bible affirms the goodness of creation, beginning with the very first chapter in Genesis which says:

> *So God created humankind in his image,*
> *In the image of God he created them;*
> *Male and female he created them.* [1:27]

What does it mean to be created in the image of God? The words "in the image of God" have been the subject of enormous amounts of discussion over the centuries. Here are some of the things that it means:

- Being created in the image of God means that we are part of God's good creation. We do sin, we do fail, we do make mistakes. But the image of God is in each of us, and that image is good, just as all of creation is good.

  When you are feeling disappointed in yourself or are unhappy about something you have done or failed to do, remember that you were created in the image of God. Whatever mistakes you may make don't change the reality that you are part of God's good creation. More than one person has said: "God don't make no junk!"

- Being created in the image of God means that we have been given the freedom to make choices. Our minds and our abilities permit far more options for our lives than birds, animals, reptiles, or plants have. We can choose to be kind or to be cruel, to love or to hate, to forgive or to hold grudges. We can even choose to ignore the reality of God or of what God wants us to do with our lives.

  And of course this means that we make choices about sexuality. Sex in the animal world is on the basis of instinct more than of choice. Many of us choose to neuter the dogs and cats we have as pets in part because the instinct to have intercourse is so strong in them that our homes could be overrun with puppies and kittens.

I remember a time in my childhood when we had one female cat. She was an indoor–outdoor cat, free to socialize around the neighborhood in the small town in which my family lived. She was not spayed, and she apparently liked to party with male cats! A year later, we had 22 cats as the result of our own population explosion! She had kittens who also had kittens who had kittens. We worked hard at finding homes for all the cats, and we spent a lot of money getting cats neutered.

Thank goodness we are not as driven by instinct as cats! While we certainly have instincts that cause us to be sexually attracted to some persons more than to other persons, we do not have to act on those instincts. Much of this book will talk about the factors that go into the choices we make about sexuality.

• Being created in the image of God means that God permits us to be part of the creative process. The fact that we have been created male and female means that two people together can produce a new, distinct life. That is a wonderful gift.

As human beings we take pleasure in creating things. Creativity takes a different form for each of us. Some of us like to build, some paint, some draw, some knit, some do computer graphics, some cook, and some play music. Whenever we are a part of creating or doing something new, we are joining God in the creative process.

• Being created in the image of God means that we have been given considerable responsibility for the planet on which we live. Our care of plants, animals, the air, and the water determines much of what our future will be like. The same is true for our care of one another. How we treat the people in our families, our schools, our congregations, and our neighborhoods affects the quality of life for others.

Talking about Sex

As with anything else that is important, we need to talk about our sexuality. It's unfortunate that so many people are uncomfortable talking about sex. One of the ways that people have shown their discomfort through the years has been by using all kinds of slang to talk about parts of the body and sexual activities. Virginia, snapper, box, snatch, slit, hole, twat, pussy, and cunt are all slang that some people have used for the vagina. Hammer, cock, dick, meat, and pecker are slang for the penis. Slang differs considerably around North America; the words used in California are not always the same used in Nebraska or Ontario.

In this book, I'll be using what are sometimes called the proper or technical words to refer to parts of the body and to sexual activities. I think the meaning of those words is clearer, and they have the same meaning no matter where you live. I don't want to change the words of others, though, so you will find slang in many of the quotes from teens and adults in this book.

If your friends use slang almost all the time to talk about sex, it may sometimes feel awkward for you to use the proper or technical terms. When you use the proper or technical terms, however, you convey that you are comfortable talking about these things and make it easier for others to understand what you are saying. It also makes it easier to talk with the adults in your life.

Sex and Love Are Not the Same Thing

Before going further talking about our sexuality, I want to briefly emphasize an important fact. Sex and love are not the same thing. Sex and love certainly are related, but we get into all kinds of trouble when we start to think of them as being identical. For example:

- The fact that you love someone doesn't mean you have to have sex with that person. Don't buy the argument that you should have sexual intercourse or any other behavior with someone to show that you really love that person.
- People sometimes have sex with people they do not love. Afterwards, they start to feel guilty and try to convince themselves that perhaps they really did love the person. That can lead to people staying in relationships and even getting married more on the basis of physical attraction than on the basis of love.

Influences on Our Sexuality

Several factors influence our sexuality, the way in which we relate to others as males and females. It's important for us to be aware of those influences. Some of the most important ones include:
(1) Parents, teachers, and other important adults.
(2) Friends.
(3) The Internet and other media.
(4) Religious influences.
(5) Our own thoughts, feelings, and decisions.

Parents, Teachers, and Other Important Adults

Our parents influence us right from the start. How our parents express their own sexuality affects us. We observe how they act as male or as female and how they interact with members of the same sex and members of the opposite sex. We learn how they behave toward each other and how they show their love. We learn about feelings they have about being male or female and about relationships.

When I surveyed teenagers around the United States, most of them said that their parents were the single most important influence on their values and behaviors in the area of sexuality. Many of those teens were frustrated because their parents weren't more comfortable talking with them about sexuality, but they appreciated the guidance they did receive.

Other significant adults in our lives may also have an influence on us. Many of us remember a teacher, a grand-parent, an aunt or uncle, a minister, a rabbi, or another person whose opinions and values were important to us. Here are some comments from teenagers:

My mother still has more impact on my life than any other person. It made a big difference in my life when she told me why she thought you should wait until married to have sex. But she also told me about birth control and was really open with me. Female Teen

I just love being around my grandmother and my grand-father. They are always so kind to each other. I see how much they can count on each other, and I think,

23

that's how a marriage ought to be. My grandfather is such a gentle person—a really good model of how a man should be. Male Teen

My mom and dad got divorced when I was twelve. I've mainly lived with Dad, who never got married again. I have this teacher in high school, Mrs. Williams, who is like another Mom to me. I can talk with her about anything. I often talk to her about things with guys that Dad would just find awkward. Female Teen

Friends

We can't help but be influenced by our friends. We spend a lot of time with them and do a lot of sharing about how we feel and what we believe. Groups of friends often share the same opinions about what is and what isn't okay to do sexually. Sometimes this is because people with the same opinions are more likely to be friends. Sometimes it's because it is just easier to go along with the crowd.

Friends can give us wonderful support when life is hard and can help us work through important decisions. They aren't always, however, the best source of information about sex. In the study of teens, I learned that friends sometimes are the source of dangerous misinformation. . . .

For example, many teens had learned from their friends that you can't get HIV/AIDS or another sexually transmitted disease from oral sex. But that isn't true. Others have learned that you can't get pregnant when a girl has her period or that you can tell by looking if a person is gay. Those aren't true either.

Value your friends, but always test the factual information you get from them.

The Internet and Other Media

The Internet, television, movies, books, and magazines all have a big impact on our sexuality. Commercials and advertisements are constantly telling us what products we need to buy to make ourselves look better and be sexier to others. Some television shows give the impression that life revolves around one sexual relationship after another.

One of the most controversial aspects of the Internet and other media is sexually explicit material. For many adults, these materials serve as a stimulant for sexual arousal. Most teenagers have seen some erotic materials, especially over the Internet. Some erotica crosses over the line into pornography, material that is so obscene it is illegal to buy or download from the Internet. Some seek it out primarily because of curiosity. What is it? What strange things do people do? What does it feel like to see pictures of naked people? Of people having intercourse?

Some teens try to learn about sexuality through these sexually explicit materials. They are especially likely to do this if their congregation, school, and parents haven't given them good information. The kinds of sexually explicit material found in some adult magazines and on the Internet have the purpose of entertaining rather than educating. These materials often give unrealistic and distorted ideas about sexuality. They are often sexist, showing men dominating and taking advantage of women. For some people, the use of those magazines and websites can become a compulsion, which may keep them from healthy relationships with real people.

Television shows, movies, and the Internet often give us opportunities to compare our bodies to the bodies of others. Unfortunately, the bodies most often portrayed in the media aren't necessarily "normal." The media tend to use actors and models who are very attractive, but the media's definition of attractiveness is fairly narrow. Actresses tend to be extremely thin, and actors tend to be well muscled. Sexually explicit magazines and websites generally present bodies with extreme proportions: large breasts and large penises. Thus if you compare yourself to movie stars, models, or x-rated stars, you may be making comparisons with a rather narrow range of body types.

Having shared those qualifications, it's also important to say that there are some wonderful television shows, movies, and Internet sites. In fact the last chapter in this book will direct you to some excellent Internet sites for more information about sexuality.

Religious Influences

Sexuality is a good gift from a loving God. The Bible, the congregation, a minister or rabbi, youth teachers, and advisors can all be sources of help in understanding your sexuality.

In the *Faith Matters* study that I did, teens who are involved in churches were asked questions about the importance of their faith:

- 70.5% said their faith is very important to them, and another 23.3% said their faith is fairly important to them. Only 4.9% said their faith is fairly unimportant, and a very small 1.4% said it is not important at all.

- 95.3% said they pray daily or at least weekly.

- 90.2% said their faith affects the decisions they make in their daily lives.

Here are some statements from teens about their faith and congregational life:

My faith is the most important thing in the world to me. . . The church matters more to me than school or sports or television or anything else. My mother almost died from cancer two years ago. The church was really there for my family. I can't tell you how many times the pastor and people in the congregation came to see us and prayed for us and even brought meals to us. They made the faith come alive. Female–United Methodist Church

I had been turned off on the church for years. But I started getting active in Youth for Christ, and in time I started going to church again with a friend from that group. I've turned my life over to Christ, and it's changed everything. I still screw up, but I'm becoming a better person. My temper's too short, and my mouth's too big, but I keep doing better with the help of Jesus. Male–Nondenominational Church

I got in such an awful depression that I was ready to kill myself. I was sitting in the car in the garage, with the door shut, and I was ready to turn the car on. My Mom would have found me in the morning. But as I was

starting to turn the key, it's like I heard this voice speaking to me in my head. It told me that I was loved and that God wanted me to serve him with my life. It scared the crap out of me. I couldn't go ahead and start the car. Male–Assembly of God

I hated the idea of going to Hebrew school. I thought it would be so boring, and what was I going to do with Hebrew? Become a rabbi? I don't think so. Then I got the surprise of my life. Hebrew school made God become real for me. I started seeing how my faith could affect and help every single thing in my life. I am so thankful for the difference that it makes. Male–Synagogue

The youth group in this church is where all my real friends are. I feel a little strange sometimes because I'm not as sure about my faith as the others in the group. Why did Jesus have to die for us to be saved? Why would God require that if God is so loving? Would a God who loves us condemn all the Jews and Buddhists to hell? The church is important to me, but I can't buy the whole package. Female–African Methodist Episcopal

Even before my first communion, the Church was very important to me. I attended our parish school until I was ready to start high school, and that helped me. The teachers were all religious, and they helped us see that faith was a part of everything that we do. I'm glad to be in a public school now, but I'll always be thankful for St. John's. Female–Roman Catholic

I used to think of being Jewish as more of a cultural thing than a religious thing. My parents aren't all that religious, but they wanted me to go to Hebrew School. We have this wonderful rabbi and great instructor, and they changed my life. I see God as the center of my life now. And I think that the way faith has become so important to me has made a difference in the lives of my parents. We talk about things we never did before. Female–Synagogue

If your faith is extremely important to you, as it was to most of the young people in the *Faith Matters* study, then it only makes sense that it should be an important part of your sexual decisions.

Your Own Thoughts, Feelings, and Decisions

You must decide how much importance to give the example of your parents and other adults, the opinion of your friends, the influence of the media, and your relationship with God as you make sexual decisions. No one else can do that for you. My hope is that studying the pages of this book will make you want to give strong weight to your relationship with God.

As you continue reading the book, you'll find that I have inserted a number of exercises and questions to encourage you to think about the decisions that you make. In some instances, I'll say very clearly what my own opinion is about particular decisions and topics. For the most part, however, I am more interested in giving you information, asking helpful questions, and trusting you to make good decisions.

There is a tendency for those of us who are adults to want teenagers to do what we say they should do. Obviously you want to pay careful attention to what people like your parents, your minister or rabbi, and other caring adults say. Ultimately, however, you are responsible for your own life and your own relationship with God. You must determine for yourself what is right and what is wrong at a particular point in life.

Remembering that Sexuality Is More than Sex

As shared at the start of this chapter, reducing the focus of our thinking from sexuality to sexual intercourse can cause us to:

- Miss the reality that how we feel about ourselves, our relationships, and our bodies is part of our sexuality–and how we care for our bodies is part of our sexuality.

- Miss the importance of relationships in healthy sexuality. We are sexual beings in the midst of all our relationships–not just when dating or engaging in sexual behaviors.

- Forget that there are many forms of sexual activity in addition to intercourse. Masturbation, kissing, flirting, and massaging are all sexual behaviors, as are fondling and oral sex.

- Miss the reality that there is a spiritual dimension
to sexuality which goes beyond the prohibition of
certain behaviors and includes recognizing that
sexuality is one of God's gifts!

Thinking about Your Own View of Sexuality

Take a few minutes to assess the influences on your own
view of sexuality and on the sexual decisions that you have
made or may be making in the future. Respond to each of the
following statements using these symbols:

SA = Strongly Agree
A = Agree
D = Disagree
SD = Strongly Disagree

_____ 1. My parents are a major influence on my sexual values
and decisions.

_____ 2. Just watching my parents and other adults has
taught me a lot about male and female roles.

_____ 3. There is absolutely no way that I am going to talk
about sex with my parents unless they tie me in a
chair and make me.

_____ 4. My friends, for the most part, have a healthy view of
sexuality.

_____ 5. I need to be careful not to let my friends have too
much influence on my sexual values and behaviors.

_____ 6. I have to admit that I'm curious about some of the
sexually explicit sites on the Internet.

_____ 7. I've learned some things about sex from the Internet
and other media that have been helpful to me.

_____ 8. Before starting to read this book, I haven't thought
very much about how my faith in God should relate to
my sexual decisions.

_____ 9. My congregation could be doing more to help teens relate their faith to sexual decision-making.

_____ 10. I am very clear about what I think it is okay and not okay to do sexually.

Chapter Four
Health and Appearance

I know the Bible teaches that we were made in the image of God. Well, if I'm in that image, then I guess God's pretty average because that's what I am. I look okay, but I'm never going to be the one that boys turn in the hall to stare at. . . . I wouldn't want to be like a couple of my friends who will do anything to keep their weight down. My friend Beth has an eating disorder. I'm so worried about her. . . . It wouldn't be a problem except for my wanting some great looking guy to take an interest in me. Why do I want that? I feel good about myself, and I'm average. Why can't I feel okay about a guy who's average? Female–Evangelical Covenant Church

Most of us have some mixed feelings about our bodies. We know deep down that there are more important things in life than physical appearance, but we don't always act that way. The female teen quoted above has some disappointments with her own appearance. She would also like to have a great-looking guy take an interest in her, even though she feels awkward about that.

The way our society emphasizes physical appearance, we can begin to feel that unless we have a certain type of body, style of hair, and shape of face, we won't be attractive to other people. Movies, television, the Internet, and magazines have created definitions of beauty that we compare ourselves to and nearly always come up short.

Our bodies are gifts from God. The biblical view of the body is a positive one and teaches us to respect and appreciate our bodies and the bodies of others. Remember:

> *So God created humankind in his image, in the image Of God he created them; male and female he created them.* **Genesis 1:27**

Since we were made in the image of God, our bodies are good, purposeful, and meant to be enjoyed and valued.

> *And the man and his wife were both naked, and*
> *were not ashamed.* **Genesis 2:25**

Just as Adam and Eve felt comfortable with each other's nakedness, there is no need for us to feel ashamed of our bodies when we are in a close, caring, and trusting relationship. The Song of Solomon celebrates the physical attraction between two people.

> *Your lips are like a crimson thread, and your mouth*
> *is lovely. Your cheeks are like halves of a pomegranate*
> *behind your veil. . . . Your two breasts are like two*
> *fawns, twins of a gazelle, that feed among the lilies.*
> **Song of Solomon 4:3, 5**

Now you may not think that a crimson thread, pomegranate halves, and fawns are the best comparisons for a person's body! But the person speaking in the Song of Solomon obviously meant these as high compliments.

The apostle Paul reminds us that God is present in each person and that we should treat ourselves and others with respect:

> *Do you not know that you are God's temple, and that*
> *God's spirit dwells in you?* **1 Corinthians 3:16**

The body is God's temple. Some of us may wish God's temple had been designed slightly differently than it has been, but the truth is that our bodies are remarkable. And each person's body is unique. No two of us look exactly the same.

Changes as People Grow

Because of the way we were created, we go through many changes. Our bodies can be unpredictable. Sometimes they change so fast we don't know what is happening to us, and sometimes it seems to take forever for changes to happen. This is especially true of puberty, the time during adolescence when our bodies reach sexual maturity. During this period, some changes are experienced by both males and females, such as increased sweating and oiliness of the skin, and an often rapid increase in height and weight. Most changes are different for each sex.

Changes in puberty for females: During puberty, girls experience a development of the breasts and a widening of the hips. Hair begins to grow in the armpits and on the lower abdomen and vulva. This pubic hair is at first straight and fine and later becomes kinky and coarse. Some girls notice hair between their breasts or around their nipples. This is perfectly normal. The first period or menarche [pronounced men-ar-key] usually occurs after these other changes have begun.

The first appearance of breast budding occurs around the age of nine or ten for many girls, and the average age for the first period is around twelve. Those averages, however, can be very misleading. These changes can take place across a fairly broad age span. Perhaps a fourth of girls will begin some changes as early as the third grade, and the first period can come as early as ten years of age or as late as sixteen. The next section talks about menstruation, which is one of the biggest changes.

Some girls worry that their breasts are too small or too large, or wonder if they will ever start developing. Breast size is determined by genetics: looking at your mother, aunts, and grandmother will give you an idea of where you will probably end up. Short of surgery, you can't change your breast size. One of the young women in the *Faith Matters* study said this:

> *As far as breast size goes, I think most of us girls*
> *want what we don't have. If we have big breasts,*
> *then we think we should have small ones like a*
> *fashion model. If we have small breasts, we think*
> *we should have big ones like those on the websites*
> *my brother goes to visit. The good news is that*
> *there are guys who like small breasts and guys who*
> *like big breasts–and most guys just like breasts.*
> *You should like yourself, like how God made you.*
> *When you like yourself, other people usually like*
> *you too.*

Changes in puberty for males: Boys also experience growth of pubic and body hair during puberty. Hair appears on the face and on other parts of the body. The testes or testicles begin to grow and the skin of the scrotum [the sac containing the testes] darkens in color. Along with an often rapid increase in height comes a lengthening and thickening of the penis. Pubic hair becomes thicker and coarser. The voice deepens, causing temporary problems in managing the pitch of the voice. Hair begins to grow in the armpits and above the upper lip and around the penis, usually between the ages of twelve and fourteen.

When a male gets sexually excited, the tissues in his penis become filled with blood, and his penis grows larger and becomes hard. This is called an erection. During puberty, boys may have erections rather frequently, sometimes at unexpected and embarrassing moments; and the erection may or may not be related to a sexual feeling.

Boys experience their first ejaculation during puberty because the hormones in the body have signaled the testes or testicles to start producing sperm. Sperm are male reproductive cells and travel from the testes. The seminal vesicles and the prostate gland produce fluid that is mixed with the sperm to form a white, sticky substance called semen. The semen is stored until the man reaches ejaculation: the semen is forced through the urethra and is expelled through the opening at the tip of the penis.

Ejaculation may occur during sexual intercourse, fondling of the genitals by another person, oral sex, masturbation, or in a wet dream. A wet dream, or nocturnal emission, refers to ejaculating during sleep. Nocturnal emissions are a natural, involuntary way of releasing stored semen.

The average age for first ejaculation is fourteen, but the normal range is anywhere from twelve to eighteen. Some males may notice a slight enlargement of the breasts during puberty, which is normal and temporary. It does not mean a boy is "turning into a girl" or anything about masculinity. If you are bothered about this, talk to your physician. If it lasts more than a year-and-a-half, be sure to get it checked out.

Many boys and some men feel that the amount of pubic hair, other body hair, and the size of the penis are indications of manhood. This is unfortunate because these things actually have nothing to do with masculinity or pleasing a sexual partner. In fact, no matter what size a penis is in the flaccid [limp] state, most penises are very similar in size when erect.

The average flaccid [or soft] penis in an adult man is two to four inches; the average erect penis is five to seven inches. My colleague Debra Haffner tells young men that some men are "showers" [they look bigger in a flaccid state] and some men are "growers" [they get proportionately larger than boys who are bigger flaccid]. Despite the advertisements you see on the Internet and in magazines, you cannot change your penis size with pills or exercises.

Menstruation

Menstruation is the shedding of the lining of the uterus and happens in every female from the first time in puberty until menopause. Menopause comes around the age of fifty but, like the first period, can come considerably earlier or considerably later. A woman is born with all the eggs she will ever produce. During puberty, hormones in the body begin the cycle of maturing eggs for possible fertilization.

Day one of the menstrual cycle is the day menstruation begins. The menstrual flow is not made up entirely of blood, but also of broken down cells and mucus that are part of the inner lining of the uterus. Each period lasts from two to eight days, with four to six being the average. Stress and illness can affect the length of the menstrual cycle.

During menstruation, women need to use pads [sanitary napkins] or tampons to absorb the flow from the vagina. Pads are usually held in place by adhesive strips. They should be changed as often as needed, which may be every three or four hours depending on the heaviness of the flow.

Many women feel tampons are more convenient to use than napkins. Tampons aren't bulky and, since they are worn internally, permit any kind of activity. They are made of highly absorbent material and are placed inside the vagina to absorb the flow before it leaves the body. Tampons can't get lost inside the body because the cervix blocks the other end of the vagina.

Toxic shock syndrome [TSS] is a disease caused by bacteria. Symptoms can include high fever, vomiting, and diarrhea. Many of the people who develop this are women who use tampons, especially if the tampon is not changed often. About five out of 100,000 women develop this condition. That's about half of what the rate was in the early 1980s, but instances have been increasing in recent years. If you want to be safe, change tampons frequently and use a pad for a part of each period.

There are many myths about menstruation that have been around for a long time. Here are some statements that are **not** true:

Myth: *A woman can't take a bath or go swimming during her period.* A woman can and should take a bath or shower during her period just like any other day. The use of a tampon makes swimming perfectly possible.

Myth: *Every woman needs to use a douche regularly.* A douche is a liquid solution, available in stores, that some women use to flush out the vagina. The vagina naturally keeps itself clean and healthy, so a douche is generally not needed. Frequent douching upsets the normal acidic balance of the vagina.

All women have some vaginal discharge. Moisture and mucus are naturally secreted by glands and membranes in the cervix and vaginal walls to help keep the vagina clean and moist. This normal discharge is clear or slightly whitish, turning yellow as it dries. It feels slippery and shouldn't be irritating or have an unpleasant odor. The amount of these normal secretions greatly increases during certain days of the menstrual cycle and during sexual excitement.

A discharge is abnormal if it causes itching, causes swelling, causes irritation, has a foul odor, or is a different color than the normal discharge. Those symptoms are probably signs of vaginal infection. Such infections are common and should be treated by a doctor. It is important to check with a doctor because some discharges may be caused by sexually transmitted disease. To help prevent vaginal infections:

-   Wash the entire vulva area regularly. Feminine hygiene sprays and strongly scented soaps may be irritating. Do not use other people's towels or washcloths.

-   Keep the vulva dry. Pat the area dry after bathing and wear clean underwear with a cotton [not nylon] crotch for greater absorbency.

- When you wipe yourself after going to the bathroom, always wipe from front to back. This practice keeps bacteria in the anus from getting to the vagina or urethra.

- If you are having sexual intercourse, be very sure your partner keeps his genitals clean, does not have a sexually transmitted disease, and uses a condom. Urination before and after intercourse will help keep urinary tract infections to a minimum.

Myth: *A woman can't have intercourse during her period* This is a matter of individual preference. Some women notice a stronger sexual drive before and during their period. Intercourse is in no way unhealthy during menstruation for the woman or her partner.

Myth: *It is impossible to get pregnant during menstruation.* Though pregnancy is unlikely during menstrualtion, it can happen. A woman's monthly cycle, especially during her teen years, can be irregular. A woman can never be absolutely certain when ovulation occurs.

Myth: *Virgins can't use tampons* Virginity is defined in various ways but traditionally means not having had sexual intercourse. The presence or absence of the hymen [flexible tissue surrounding or partially covering the entrance to the vagina] is not proof of virginity. Some girls are born without a hymen, and others have their hymen stretched by strenuous activity. Tampons can also stretch the hymen slightly, but this has nothing to do with virginity.

Myth: *Cramps and mood changes are just psychological.* Some people believe that cramps are all in the head–that there are no physical reasons for them. Although emotions and attitudes related to menstruation can affect how a woman feels during her period, menstrual pain is not merely psychological. The reasons for cramps are not fully understood, but they are probably related to contractions of the uterus and changes in the blood supply to the uterus. Cramps are often worse in the first years after you get your period and are almost always gone after childbirth.

Remedies which may help to ease cramping include: a warm bath or heating pad, exercise, pain relievers such as naproxen or ibuprofen, or drugstore medications made specifically for menstrual discomfort. If severe cramps continue, a doctor should be consulted.

"Mood swings" can also be caused by changing hormone levels. Many women experience what has been called PMS or premenstrual syndrome. This syndrome includes symptoms like irritability, tension, and depression, as well as weight gain, headaches, diarrhea, breast tenderness, and a heavy feeling in the abdomen. If these symptoms are severe, it may be the result of a hormone deficiency.

Physical Attractiveness and Health

As shared earlier, our bodies are gifts from God, and we should be thankful for them. Some of us, of course, would be more thankful if we could change a few things! Take a couple of minutes to respond to the following statements about your body before continuing with the chapter:

How I Feel about My Body

1. Overall I would describe the way I feel about my body and my physical appearance in this way [choose one]:
   a) I am definitely happy with my body.
   b) I am happy with my body but would really like to make some improvements.
   c) I am somewhat unhappy with my body.
   d) I am definitely unhappy with my body.

2. When shopping for a swimming suit, I ____ [choose as many as apply].
   a) select primarily for comfort.
   b) select primarily for appearance.
   c) select a sexy look.
   d) think carefully about what my boyfriend or girlfriend would like.
   e) think that I would rather be having a root canal.

3. Here's what I think about the possibility of having some kind of cosmetic surgery [choose as many as apply]:
   a) I'd do it in a flash if I could afford it.

38

b) I don't think I'm old enough yet to consider such a thing.
c) I feel like I'm the way God made me, and I shouldn't have a plastic surgeon change it.
d) I'd be embarrassed to let any of my friends know I'd done it.
e) I think the right change could make me feel better about myself.

4. When thinking about a decision to go out with another person, here's how I feel about the physical attractiveness of that person [choose as many as apply]:
a) The physical attractiveness of that person is one of the most important factors in a decision to go out.
b) The physical attractiveness of that person is important but not as important as some other things like values and personality.
c) The physical attractiveness of that person is not important at all.
d) I want to think that physical attractiveness is not important, but I'm not sure I could handle some serious problem like a facial deformity or a serious physical challenge.
e) Some very attractive people are so full of themselves that it could be a turnoff to me.

5. When thinking about a decision to spend the rest of my life with another person, here's how I feel about the physical attractiveness of that person [choose as many as apply]:
a) The physical attractiveness of that person is one of the most important factors in a decision to marry.
b) The physical attractiveness of that person is important but not as important as some other things like values and personality.
c) The physical attractiveness of that person is not important at all.
d) I want to think that physical attractiveness is not important, but I'm not sure I could handle some serious problem like a facial deformity or a serious physical challenge.
e) Some very attractive people are so full of themselves that it could be a turnoff to me.
f) I don't think physical attractiveness is as likely to influence me in selecting a person to marry as it is in the initial decision to go out on a date.

We asked the teens in the *Faith Matters* study to choose from one of four options to describe how happy they were with their bodies. There were significant differences between the way that teenage males and teenage females feel about their bodies.

- Among the females in the study, 61.9% were somewhat or definitely unhappy with their bodies; 19.5% were happy but still wanted some improvement; and only 18.6% were happy without qualification.

- The comparable figures for males were 48.5% somewhat or definitely unhappy; 17.2% happy but wanting some improvement, and 24.3% happy without qualification.

Almost twice as many girls as boys were "definitely unhappy" with their bodies. Still, many boys are unhappy and want changes. Some of the teens had very strong feelings about their appearance and the importance that attractiveness played in their lives:

I hate my body. I diet, I exercise, I do everything right. But it doesn't make any difference. I still have ten pounds that won't go away, and that keeps me from looking like I should. . . . Two of my friends have bigger weight problems than I do and think I shouldn't complain. But I don't want to look like this. Female–Missouri Synod Lutheran

White people are the ones with the problem about weight. Black people aren't as concerned. We look more at what's in a person's heart. This is one of the differences between the races. I get so ripped because my white girlfriends are always worried about their weight and their muscles. Get a life, people. Female–Roman Catholic Church

I was a fat baby, and I'm a fat high school student. I'm smart. I'm funny. I know lots of girls who like to be with me and ask my opinions. They wouldn't go on a date with me though. I don't look good enough. They have to see themselves as being able to get someone better than me to ask them out. Male–Southern Baptist Church

I had a birthmark on my face until three years ago. Then a plastic surgeon used this new method to help me grow a balloon of skin on the side of my face. I went into hiding for the summer while the skin was growing. Then he

used my own skin to fix the birthmark. The difference was awesome. I look so good now, and it feels so good. But I know who my real friends are. My real friends are the ones who liked me before the surgery. These guys who wouldn't give me a second look before the surgery, I have no second look for them now. In one way I'm so happy with how I look, but in another I'm not. When I had the ugly blotch on my face, it was easy to know who cared about the real me, the me that no one sees on the surface. Female–Presbyterian Church U.S.A.

I looked like such a dork in middle school. Now I've grown more, and I've been lifting weights and running. My sister says I look like a hunk. She's like drop dead beautiful, so I guess she should know, but I still don't see myself that way. I keep thinking I must look like a dork. I have this low self-confidence in talking to girls that I can't seem to get past. Male–Synagogue

I worry about my sister so much. She was a little heavy until the summer of her freshman year. Then she went on this diet and started running every day. She looks so hot now. That should be a good thing, but down inside she still sees herself as pudgy. She wants affection from guys so much that she'll do almost anything to get it. She doesn't have enough pride in herself, and she has the rep of being "easy." It makes me feel so bad for her. Appearance has so much to do with everything. Male–Friends Meeting

I don't think appearance is as important to women as it is to men. But there are some basics. There's this guy that I used to go out with who had skanky breath most of the time. I'd hold my breath to kiss him so I didn't gag. I finally told him about it, and I hurt his feelings so much that he cried. I was so sorry, but I thought he ought to know. Female–Church of Jesus Christ of Latter Day Saints

The African-American teens in the sample were more likely than the other ethnic groups to feel good about their physical appearance. The female quoted in this chapter is not the only black person in the study to express frustration with the emphasis that white people put on weight and appearance.

Seventy-seven percent of the females and 39% of the males in the study have been on a diet sometime in the last year. The figures for African Americans were lower but are still high [55% of females and 27% for males]. Six percent of the females and 1.5% of the males acknowledge that they have or have had an eating disorder. This was a request for self-identification, so the actual number may be higher. Almost all the teens of both sexes acknowledge that they know someone with an eating disorder.

Cosmetic surgical procedures have become increasingly common among teenagers. According to the American Society of Plastic Surgeons, 331,886 procedures were done on Americans 18 and younger in 2003 which was a 48% jump over the year. A cleft palate, buck teeth, big stick-out ears, or a badly deformed nose may be things worth fixing, but many plastic surgeons themselves are uncomfortable doing other kinds of procedures on teenagers. Operations like breast augmentation, lipsuction, and rhinoplasty should generally only be performed on fully grown people. The growth in popularity of so many cosmetic surgical procedures among young people seems reflective of an unhealthy obsession with a particular kind of appearance in our society. The depiction of these procedures on television shows may also have contributed to their popularity.

We asked the teens to rate the importance of physical attractiveness and seven other characteristics in determining whether or not to date or go out with a person. There were some definite male and female differences, and those changed with year in school. A characteristic marked "one" would be the most important; one marked "eight" would be the least important. This table shows the average rank given to appearance:

**Ranking of Appearance from Eight Characteristics
In Deciding to Date or Go Out with a Person**

	Males	Females
Freshmen	Five	Four
Sophomores	Four	Four
Juniors	Three	Five
Seniors	Two	Six

The older females placed less importance on physical appearance than the younger females in contrast to the older males who placed more importance on appearance than the younger males. In any exercise like this, there is the possibility, of course, that some teens were answering as they felt they *should* rather than as they actually do feel.

How much importance should we place on the physical appearance of ourselves and of others? While the answer is going to be different for each person, it's clear that our culture as a whole puts too much importance on appearance. Magazines, television, movies, and the Internet all glorify certain kinds of physical appearance; and those end up becoming the standard for many of us. But as has been discussed earlier in this book, very few of us actually look like movie stars, so accepting those standards sets us up for failure!

The next two pages share some guidelines for people wanting to reflect on the topic of physical appearance from a religious perspective. Think about those guidelines and how following them might be helpful to your life.

Guidelines on Physical Appearance

1. Remember that God made us and loves us as we are. God doesn't feel better or worse about us because of our physical appearance.

2. God created tremendous diversity in the physical appearance of people and obviously likes diversity. We should celebrate the reality that no two of us look alike.

3. What we consider "handsome" or "beautiful" or "good-looking" is largely a matter of what we have learned to value from the media and other people. There are other cultures, for example, in which heavy people are considered more attractive than thin people.

4. A person's physical appearance has nothing to do with that person's intelligence or personality or worth. We should be very careful about making negative or positive judgments about people based on their appearance–including judgments about ourselves.

5. People with serious physical challenges, including persons in wheelchairs and persons with missing limbs, can still have fulfilling sexual relationships with others.

A junior in high school whom I interviewed in the Faith Matters *study, had been dating a girl as a sophomore when a swimming pool accident confined him to a wheelchair. While out of town at a special rehabilitation center, he wrote to her and told her to forget about him because he would only be a burden in her life. She skipped school to travel to the center and told him, "You can never be a burden to me, only a blessing. Don't write me any more silly letters." She knew what was important, and she was prepared to deal with any complications from his disability.*

6. While too much emphasis on physical appearance isn't good, many of us need to place more emphasis on our physical health! Diet, exercise, and abstaining from substances and practices that harm our bodies will unquestionably improve our lives.

7. Many of us should take the time that we spend obsessing about our physical appearance and use it to exercise and become healthier people!

8. Remember that we all change in appearance over time. Our bodies are wonderful, but they are not eternal. Through the years, people lose some muscle mass and gain wrinkles and eventually wear out. For most healthy people, that process takes many years–but it does happen. One girl in the *Faith Matters* study said this:

   Good looks are fleeting, but a rotten personality can last a lifetime. We'd better remember that when we decide who we want to date and who we want to marry. You might like how someone looks in bed, but will you like him when you look at him across the breakfast table or when depending on him to help raise children together?

9. Pray about your feelings concerning your own appearance and the appearance of others.

Physical Health

Our culture doesn't seem to place as much emphasis on personal health as on personal appearance. Consider the following facts about the health of teenagers in the United States:

• More than one-third of young people in grades 9-12 do not regularly engage in vigorous physical activity. Another third exercise in binges but not throughout the year. More teens watch two hours of television or more each day than exercise on a regular basis.

45

- The percentage of teenagers who are overweight has tripled in the last twenty years. Just one additional soft drink a day can increase the risk of obesity by almost 60%.

- One study found that teenagers today visit fast food outlets an average of four times a week. A single supersize fast food meal contains ALL the calories a typical person should consume in a whole day!

- The prevalence of diabetes among young people has increased ten-fold over the past 20 years. Much of this appears to be related to excessive sugar consumption and too many fast food meals.

- Approximately 90% of adult smokers started smoking before the age of 18. Everyday, nearly 3,000 young people under the age of 18 become regular smokers.

- Underage drinkers account for up to 20 percent of the alcohol consumed in the U.S. Four of every five teens in state juvenile justice systems were under the influence of alcohol or drugs while committing their crimes.

- Thirty-five percent of females and 15% of males in faith based institutions have had an unwanted sexual experience by the end of high school. Among teens who have had these unwanted experiences, 26.3% were using alcohol or drugs at the time.

One of the best ways to feel better about ourselves is to take care of our bodies. Doing that will probably cause us to be more attractive, and it will improve the quality of our lives in many other ways. Here's a quick overview of some things you can do to have a healthier lifestyle.

Participate in regular physical exercise–at least 30 minutes of moderate activity on at least five days per week, or 20 minutes of vigorous activity at least three times per week. Regular physical activity has beneficial effects on most [if not all] organ systems, and consequently it helps to prevent a broad range of health problems and diseases such as heart disease, diabetes, high blood pressure, colon cancer, and breast cancer.

Regular physical activity can improve your life beyond its effects on physical health. Studies have found participation in physical activity increases teens' self esteem and reduces anxiety and stress. Through its positive impact on mental health, physical activity may even help increase your capacity for learning. Spend more time exercising and less time in front of the television! Visit this website–http://aspe.hhs.gov–for further information.

Being overweight brings many health risks. While eating properly and exercising on a regular basis makes it far less likely that a person will be obese or fat, it is true that genetics make it easier for some people to remain thin than for other people to remain thin. This is not fair, but it is part of life.

Some persons are chronically underweight, often because of eating disorders like bulimia or anorexia. These are dangerous conditions that can cause permanent damage to a person's health.

If you have an eating disorder or even think you might be suffering from such a disorder, it's very important to get help. Talk to your physician, or call 1-800-762-3334 or 1-800-227-4785 for Hot Line Help.

Don't worry about going on a diet, but improve the food choices that you make. Many young people, like adults, consume more calories than needed without getting the recommended amounts of vitamins, protein, and other important nutrients. Consider these guidelines from About Pediatrics and the U.S. Department of Agriculture:

- Consume a sufficient amount of fruits and vegetables. That means at least two to four servings of fruit and three to five servings of vegetables each day.

- Be sure, during the week, to include all five vegetable subgroups: dark green, orange, legumes, starchy, and other vegetables.

- Concentrate on whole grain breads and cereals–whole wheat bread is better than white bread.

- Be very careful about sugar consumption–especially about too many soft drinks. And avoid fast food or at least limit your fast food trips to one or two a week. Don't let your meal be supersized!

One girl who participated in the *Faith Matters* study realized that she was drinking five cans of soft drinks a day. She cut back to one can a day, felt much better, and lost thirty pounds in a year without any other changes in her diet.

• When selecting meat, poultry, dry beans, and milk products, make choices that are lean, low fat, or fat-free.

• Fresh foods are better for us than processed foods. Use fresh fruits and vegetables whenever available.

• Keep your diet moderate in salt and sodium. All of us need salt and sodium, but most of us eat more than we should.

You can learn more about nutrition on the web. Here's one site that can help: http://pediatrics.about.com/od/nutrition/

Don't smoke; stop smoking if you already are. The Surgeon General reports that even by age 18, young people clearly experience adverse health effects from smoking such as reduced physical fitness, shortness of breath, coughs, more frequent respiratory illness, early development of artery disease, and slower rate of lung growth. The long-term consequences include cancer, heart disease, stroke, peripheral vascular disease, chronic bronchitis, emphysema, pregnancy complications, slower healing, facial wrinkling, eye disorders such as macular degeneration and glaucoma, and compromised immune function. Smoking shortens male smokers' lives by 13.2 years and females smokers' lives by 14.5 years.

All of those are powerful reasons not to smoke. Here's another in the words of a boy in the *Faith Matters* study:

Hey, the last thing I want to do is kiss someone who's a smoker. How gross. Who would want to do it?

A girl in the study put it this way:

If a guy is a smoker, that's a deal breaker for me. There's no way I'm every sticking my tongue in the

mouth of someone with tobacco breath. And who
wants to fall in love with someone who will die twenty
years before you because of lung cancer?

If your parents smoke, tell them this: teens whose parents do not smoke and who encourage them not to smoke are 80% less likely than others to pick up this habit. For help stopping, visit these sites: www.cfah.org/factsoflife/vol5no7.cfm and www.cancer.org.

Don't drink alcoholic beverages or use illegal drugs. There are just too many negative consequences. Over three million teenagers are out-and-out alcoholics. Several million more have a serious drinking problem that they cannot manage on their own. The three leading causes of death for 15 to 24 year olds are automobile crashes, homicides, and suicides– alcohol is a leading factor in all three.

Now I know that some of you are going to experiment with alcohol whether it's legal or not. What's even more important to me is that you never drive after you've had even one drink. If you are going to drink with friends, be sure there is a designated driver who does not drink. Never get in a car with a person who has been drinking.

Dependence on alcohol and other drugs is also associated with problems such as depression and anxiety. Teens who use alcohol are also at greater risk for unplanned sexual intercourse, sexual violence, and exposure to HIV, the virus that causes AIDS. A teenage girl in the *Faith Matters* study shared this perspective:

> *You shouldn't drink and drive. You also shouldn't*
> *drink and have sex. The decision to have sex is*
> *too important to make when you're under the influence*
> *of alcohol.*

Drug abuse is costly to our society as a whole but is especially harmful to youth. Behavior patterns that result from drug use often produce consequences such as self-degradation, loss of control, disruptive conduct, and antisocial attitudes. The effects of amphetamines, inhalants, marijuana, and MDMA (ecstasy) include: insomnia, anxiety, paranoia, aggression, depression, psychosis, memory loss, convulsions, vomiting, chronic bronchitis, grand mal seizures, stroke, cardiovascular collapse, brain damage, and death.

There's another problem with illegal drugs. If you get caught by law enforcement authorities, you can go to prison; and going to prison will for sure mess up your life. It's just not worth it.

For more information about alcohol and illegal drugs, visit: www.nida.nih.gov and www.focusas.com/alcohol.html.

In a society as obsessed as ours with personal appearance, it's almost impossible not to put too much emphasis on this part of who we are. But the Bible brings the good news that God created us and loves us as we are.

The Bible also teaches us that the body is God's temple. That means that we should take good care of it. Having a healthy lifestyle will bring some improvements to our appearance, but more importantly it will improve the quality of our lives.

Chapter Five
Abstinence and Slowing Things Down

*My youth advisor told me that she'd had sex before she
was married and was sorry that she had. She didn't
think it made her an awful person, but she would have
liked herself better if she'd waited. I don't want to
make the same mistake.*
                              Female–Evangelical Lutheran Church

In spite of all the emphasis on sex in our culture and all the talk that makes it seem like everyone is having sexual intercourse, the reality is that huge numbers of teenagers are choosing not to have premarital intercourse or oral sex. In fact, the majority of teens in the *Faith Matters* study have not had either of those sexual experiences. Many people are choosing to be virgins, to abstain from intercourse or oral sex, and they are doing so without apology. They feel good about themselves because of the decision they have made. Here are some comments from teens:

*I want to be a virgin when I'm married. I want that
first night together to be the most beautiful in my life.*
Female–Church of God

*If you have sex with every person you go out with, then
what's left to share with the one person you decide to
marry?* Male–American Baptist Church

*The body is the temple of God. The Bible's clear on this.
That means that you want to use your body in a way that
is pleasing to God. Waiting until marriage for sex is part
of honoring God through the body.* Male–United Methodist
Church

*I plan to wait on marriage until I've finished college and
have a career started. I don't know if I'll wait until
then to have intercourse, but I do know I'm not ready now.
And I resent it when a guy thinks he has it coming because
he pays for a movie and pizza.* Female–Roman Catholic
Church

If Mary was a virgin when Jesus was conceived, wasn't Joseph too? Our youth pastor says that virginity is for males and females. I wouldn't want to marry a person who had intercourse with other people, and I need to meet my own standard. Male–Presbyterian Church U.S.A.

Virginity is a choice. You don't owe anyone an explanation. I choose it to honor God, my parents, and myself. I don't think it makes me better than people who make a different choice, but I also don't think it makes me weird. Female–Synagogue

Abstaining from sex as a teenager does not necessarily mean that a person will wait until marriage to have intercourse.

In the Faith Matters *study, 41.7% of the ninth grade females and 32.3% of the ninth grade males indicated that they are committed to waiting until they are married before having sexual intercourse. That percentage of agreement declines with each year in school. Among twelfth graders, 22.8% of the females and 17.6% of the males are committed to waiting until they are married before having sexual intercourse.*

That means 77% of these young women and 82% of these young men are considering the possibility that they will have sex before marriage.

The fact that the majority of the teens are not committing themselves to waiting until marriage before having intercourse does not mean that they take this activity lightly. Ninety-two percent of the teens in the *Faith Matters* study indicated agreement with this statement: "Sexual intercourse should only happen between people who have a commitment to each other." Many of the teens did not say that sexual intercourse only belongs in marriage, but there is nothing casual about the view of most of these teens toward intercourse.

Pledges

A movement called True Love Waits has been especially popular. That movement seeks to have teens sign this pledge:

*Believing that true love waits, I make a commitment
to God, myself, my family and my friends, my future
mate and my future children to be sexually abstinent
from this day until the day I enter a biblical marriage
relationship.*

True Love Waits originated in the Southern Baptist denomination but has become a movement which is not exclusive to any denomination. About 90 organizations participate in this ministry, including denominations and crisis pregnancy centers, as well as some popular Christian recording artists. In our survey, we found that youth in many different Christian denominations have participated in this movement, including Roman Catholic, United Methodist, Southern Baptist, Disciples of Christ, Episcopal, Missouri Synod Lutheran, Evangelical Lutheran, and Pentecostal teens. While congregations cooperate and are generally the driving force behind the movement in a particular geographical area, the program itself sometimes comes to life through the school system and will reach teens who are not connected with any faith-based institution as well as those who are active in congregations.

Although 19% of the youth responding to the *Faith Matters* survey have taken a pledge to remain a virgin until marriage, that group was not any more or less likely than others in the study to have had sexual intercourse or to have experienced or caused pregnancy. The promotion of abstinence by the congregation does have an impact, when combined with other characteristics as noted later in this book. This doesn't mean that virginity pledges are not worthwhile, but apparently they don't have as much impact on youth who are already highly active in the church or synagogue.

Some teens who have made virginity pledges have nevertheless had intercourse and even become pregnant or impregnated someone. Here are a few comments from teens in the *Faith Matters* study who are in that situation:

*At times I have a lot of guilt because I made the pledge
and then broke it. I didn't know how hard it was going
to be to keep the pledge. I don't so much feel bad about
having sex as I do about breaking my word. I would
be sick if my parents and pastor knew what I've done.*
Female–Southern Baptist Church

*I felt like we were forced into making the pledge. All
these cards got put up on the bulletin board in the church.
Our church isn't that big. If your card didn't go up there,
people were going to know. You had to make the pledge
or catch s - - - from the pastor and your parents. Most
of us knew it didn't mean anything.* Male–Missouri
Synod Lutheran Church

*I broke the pledge, but I'm still glad I made it. It kept
me from having sex too early. Before my boyfriend and
I had sex, I thought about it and prayed. I feel like God
released me from my promise. My boyfriend and I are
in love, and we're going to get married. Having sex with
him isn't the same as it would have been with anyone else.*
Female–Disciples of Christ

*I broke the pledge, and I'm sorry I did. I thought the two
of us were in love and were going to get married. Turns
out he was having sex with another person the nights we
weren't together. I thought he was doing homework. . . .
True Love Waits talks about being able to have a second
chance. You can pray to God and like become a virgin
again. That's what I'm trying to do.* Female–Church of
God.

Perhaps you know people who have taken a virginity pledge.
Perhaps you have taken one yourself. Such commitments can
be very valuable to a young person, but there are some
important things to keep in mind:

• Don't make a virginity pledge because everyone else is
doing it [just like you shouldn't have sex because everyone else is doing it]. Make sure it is a commitment
that is right for you and that you have arrived at through
careful thought and prayer.

• Remember that there is a difference between saying that
a person is not going to have sexual intercourse as a
teenager or in high school and saying that a person is
not going to have intercourse until marriage. In our
time, the average age of people getting married for the
first time has increased and is now 26 for men and 25
for women in the U.S. and 29 for men and 27 for women
in Canada. That's a long time to wait. As shared earlier,
many of the teens in the *Faith Matters* study see sexual

intercourse as a serious step that requires a committed relationship, but they don't necessarily see waiting until they are married. If you make a pledge, think about what you are pledging. . . . until marriage or until out of high school?

- You also need to think about what you are agreeing to abstain from! Just sexual intercourse? What about oral sex? What about fondling each other to orgasm? Be clear with yourself and with God about what your pledge means.

- If you have made a pledge and have broken it, remember that God does forgive us when we fail to keep our commitments. Don't continue to kick yourself for not having lived up to the promise. Learn from the experience and be more careful about major commitments in the future. And if you are having sexual intercourse, be sure to use contraception and condoms. Coming chapters in this book will have more to say about avoiding pregnancy and disease.

Slowing Things Down

Sexuality is a very powerful part of our lives, and sexual relationships are complex. The responses to the *Faith Matters* study show that many young people are pushed into or move into oral sex and sexual intercourse before they are ready to do so. There were also many young people who do not have sexual intercourse but are very frustrated because they get sexually aroused and feel there is nothing they can do about it. Here are what a couple of young people said:

I really love my guy and want to express my love to him, but I don't feel ready for intercourse. I may not want to do it until I get married. It gets damned frustrating though to get aroused and have trouble controlling yourself.
Female–Synagogue

The fellows I hang with talk like kissing and intercourse are the only options. So you start kissing and then you start touching and then you feel like you have to have intercourse or your balls will fall off and you'll lose your mind. I know it doesn't have to be that way, but I don't

know what to do about it. Male–African Methodist
Episcopal Church

From a religious perspective, sexual relationships need to
develop gradually as people better understand each other, better
communicate with each other, and better like each other. There
are a lot of options besides kissing and having intercourse. In
fact, a whole lot should happen between the time that a couple
kisses and the time that same couple experiences intercourse.
Part of the reason that so many responding to the *Faith Matters*
study felt awkward and did not enjoy intercourse is that they
were not ready for that level of intimacy.

Sexual intercourse, as will be discussed later in this book, is
a rather complicated way of expressing love for each other. It
requires a great deal of comfort with each other; familiarity with
one's own body and the body of the other person; and the ability
to communicate rather well. Unless those conditions are all
met, sexual intercourse will not be a great experience.

And sexual intercourse is not just a physical relationship.
There is a spiritual dimension that is always present. When a
man and a woman have intercourse, their relationship has been
changed. It may have been changed for the better; it may have
been changed for the worse. If the intercourse grows out of
genuine love and respect for each other and reflects tenderness
and kindness, then the change in the relationship is likely to be
a positive one. If the intercourse grows out of physical
attraction alone and involves the desire of one or both partners
to "control" the other, then the relationship has been changed
for the worse.

**Those are some of the reasons that all major religious
traditions have urged that sexual intercourse be confined to
marriage relationships. It is within the institution of
marriage that couples have opportunity for the kind of deep
knowledge of each other that insures the sexual relationship
will be a good one.**

Even if you are not committed to waiting until you are
married for intercourse, moving directly from a good night kiss
to intercourse or oral sex is not the way to build a healthy
sexual relationship. Consider the following thoughts:

1. Sexual relationships need to be developed in a gradual way, over a period of time. Couples should not participate in sexual activity before having reached a comparable level in their ability to communicate with each other and to show concern for each other.

Regardless of age, couples should not move beyond the level of light kissing the first several times that they go out. For younger teens who have had little or no dating experience, this level should not be passed for a long time. Older, more experienced teens should consider staying at this level until they have developed some comfort in talking with each other and have talked about their mutual values.

Longer, more frequent kissing often comes about naturally as a couple spend more time together and become more comfortable with each other. The move to what is often called "french kissing," in which partners insert tongues in each other's mouths, is frequently accompanied by some light fondling or touching. Thus it is very important to recognize that when you move from light kissing to heavy kissing, the temptation or the desire to move to fondling will be strong.

It's hard to distinguish between hugging and light fondling. It's also hard to distinguish between light fondling and heavier fondling. But there is a lot of difference between hugging and heavy fondling. Hugging, holding each other tightly, is a normal action that often accompanies kissing. Light fondling involves touching and stroking each other and often develops to the point of massaging the breasts of the woman. Couples need to be careful because the level of arousal is quite high at this stage, and the contact should not be prolonged unless both partners feel ready to move to heavy fondling. Remember, however, that you can *stop* sexual activity at any time, no matter how aroused.

Good communication should be occurring throughout the dating relationship. It is very important not to move to heavy fondling unless you have clearly discussed what you each want and value in your expression of affection. Heavy fondling and light fondling [some call this heavy "petting" and light "petting"] are obviously relative terms. Heavy fondling as used here means fondling below the waist. The reason for being especially careful before moving to heavy fondling is that it is deeply frustrating to fondle below the waist for extended periods of time unless both partners want to fondle to the point of orgasm.

57

When couples begin stroking the penis and the vulva, the level of arousal is enormous. A couple should have consciously, verbally decided that they want to stimulate each other to orgasm before beginning fondling for an extendcd period of time. Most couples are not ready for this level of intimacy until they have been a couple for several months or longer and have had serious conversations about their values and limits. Fondling only belongs in very serious relationships.

Remember that you can enjoy a long term dating relationship and never move beyond light kissing. Our culture tries to convince you this is not true, but it is.

There are other levels of intimacy beyond heavy fondling. For many, the next level involves fondling in the nude; and many of the teens in the *Faith Matters* study have done that. The move to nudity, for most couples, should come gradually rather than abruptly. It will normally be an outgrowth of heavy fondling.

For some, nude fondling is followed by oral sex. Oral sex is an extremely intimate activity and brings with it potential exposure to HIV/AIDS and other sexually transmitted diseases. People should not move to this stage unless they have a very mature relationship and have taken precautions to lower the risk of a sexually transmitted disease. That means a condom for males and a dental dam or some other barrier for females. A dental dam is a six-inch sheet of latex to place over a woman's vulva when oral sex is performed on her. They are available at health clinics, AIDS organizations, and some drugstores. Some people think they are too thick and slip around. Alternatives include cutting a condom open and laying it flat or using non-microwave plastic wrap.

Good communication before oral sex or sexual intercourse includes a willingness to talk about the past. Consider this math exercise:
- Bob and Annie just had intercourse with each other.
- Last year they each slept with four other people. [4 + 4 = 8]
- The year before that each of those people slept with three other people. [8 X 3 = 24]
- The year before that each of those people

slept with three other people. [24 X 3 = 72]
- Thus Bob and Annie have slept with people who have slept with other people, making a total of 104 [8 + 24 + 72 = 104].
- That means that the risk of a sexually transmitted disease relates to all 104 of those people, not just to Bob and Annie.

If Bob and Annie fail to talk honestly with each other about the past, they will not be aware of the risks they are taking.

Some people will never choose to have oral sex. It's a matter of personal preference. The other stages, however, should usually have happened before people move to sexual intercourse. Sexual intercourse should not happen until:

- They have a method of contraception which is acceptable to both of them or are married and are ready to have children.
- In addition to contraception, they need to be using a condom for protection against sexually transmitted disease, unless they are married and have not had intimate sexual contact with other people.
- They have shared enough experiences and feelings that they are both ready for intercourse.
- They are both certain, if unmarried, that they do not want to reserve sexual intercourse for marriage.
- They are certain, if unmarried, that having sexual intercourse will not be a problem to their spiritual lives.

My colleague Debra Haffner offers this framework for a moral, sexual relationship. The relationship should be:

- **C**onsensual
- **N**on-exploitive
- **H**onest
- **M**utually pleasurable
- **P**rotected against sexually transmitted disease, and pregnancy if penile-vaginal intercourse occurs

Those are standards that can apply to relationships of persons who are 16 years old or 60 years old. The relationship should be **consensual**, with both partners in agreement on what they want to do. That includes both partners feeling that the activity is morally acceptable. It should be **non-exploitive** with neither person taking advantage of the other. If one person is attempting to talk the other into something he or she does not want to do, it is an exploitive and unhealthy relationship. The relationship should be characterized by a deep level of **caring** for each other, so that exploitation is not an option.

The relationship should be **honest** with each person being truthful about how they feel about the other. If either person has had sexual activity with other people in the past, that information needs to be shared so that both know what risks of sexually transmitted disease may be present. The relationship should be **mutually pleasurable**, with both persons feeling good about what is happening. And there should be **protection** against sexually transmitted disease and pregnancy.

Most couples will not be in as great a hurry for sexual intercourse if they have found that they can achieve orgasm in other ways. Some people will determine that they do not want to achieve orgasm until marriage, except in private masturbation.

2. It's okay to say NO to any form of sexual expression. Don't let someone else manipulate you. Don't let someone else push you into something that you do not want, and don't be guilty of pushing someone else.

One of the major reasons for sharing so much statistical information and quotes from other teens in this book is to help you see that "normal" sexual activity for teenagers covers a very broad range. You'll discover that in the chapters that follow. People who tell you that "everyone" has oral sex or intercourse are not telling you the truth.

Many people have intercourse and other forms of sexual activity for unfortunate reasons like these:

- As an attempt to cure their loneliness.
- Out of a desire to increase popularity.
- Out of concern that they not appear homosexual.
- As a way of asserting independence from adult authority.
- In the hope of having a romantic relationship like those portrayed in movies and on television.

Those are not good reasons for sex with another person. In fact they are very bad reasons.

3. As a person committed to God, you want to remember that both you and the other person are the children of God. While sexual expression can be pleasurable and fun, sex is not just a physical matter. Your emotional life, your social life, and your spiritual life all become part of the sexual experience.

4. Whenever you begin a new dating relationship, "return to square one." Start over with a handshake or a good night kiss; don't try to pick up where you left off in your last dating relationship. You need time to know and understand the other person and to be understood by that person. You need time to develop comfort in communicating with each other. You need time to be certain how you both feel about sexual activity.

5. Remember that our culture puts lots of pressure for early sexual activity on teens and young adults. This pressure is especially hard for junior high youth. In general, junior high youth need a lot of group dating and group contact with the opposite sex before becoming involved in any kind of sexual activity. They should normally not go beyond light kissing. Most junior highs are not emotionally ready for heavier forms of sexual activity.

High school students find that classmates, the Internet, movies, and television can all create pressure for sexual activity. Don't let that pressure control what you do. Think clearly about your faith, your values, your hopes, your dreams, and your respect for yourself and the other person.

These pressures don't end with graduation from high school. In some ways the expectation of sexual activity can be even stronger on college students, people in the military, and people who have begun full-time jobs. Being older does not necessarily mean that sexual activity should come faster. While young adults have generally had more sexual experience that high school students, that doesn't change the need for clear communication with the other person and living consistently with one's faith and values.

6. Remember that all of us have trouble with negative self-images. I almost changed that sentence to say "most of us," but then I realized that the sentence is true. No matter how secure we are or how much we have accomplished, all of us have times when we have low opinions of ourselves. We may dislike certain aspects of our appearance or how we do in school or a career or how we communicate with others. We may dislike how other people tend to respond to us. We may dislike obsessive patterns of thinking that we have or our inability to be more disciplined.

We need to be careful that negative self-images do not lead us to behaviors we'll later regret. A male with a poor self-image may well seek to prove himself or feel better about himself by the sexual conquest of another person, whether he actually wants a particular sexual experience or not. A female with a poor self-image may well be afraid to say NO for fear of rejection. This is not to say that it is always the male who pushes for sex and the female who decides whether or not to "give in." Those roles can be reversed, and those roles may also be different for homosexual persons. **Self-image is not enhanced by forcing one's will on another person or by letting oneself be victimized by another person.**

Caring relationships with friends of the same sex and the opposite sex can do much to improve our self-images. When we relate honestly to others and are genuinely concerned about them, we are able to give and receive valuable affirmation which almost always results in improved self-images.

Roman Catholic theologian John Powell suggests in his book *The Christian Vision* that there are actually two people lurking inside each of us. One of those people is a wounded, hurt, angry person. That person feels that all the injustice of life is focused on himself or herself and feels horribly hurt and angry. The other person within each of us is a good, decent, caring, loving person. That person sees the best in others and the best in himself or herself. Having a healthy emotional life and healthy relationships depends directly on keeping the loving, caring person in control of one's life. Involvement in the life of your congregation and regular prayer are strong ways of keeping that person in charge!

One of the greatest gifts that comes from a loving relationship is that two people are able to more fully disclose themselves to one another. Receiving genuine affirmation makes it much easier to feel good about ourselves, easier to affirm others, and easier to keep the loving, caring self in control of life.

All of us find it easier to say NO! to sexual pressure when we learn to say YES! to the best that is within us. A person who does not want to get to know you at a deep level is not a person who cares enough to ever make a good sexual partner.

> *We are all in need of a little love and a little under-standing. And it is this love and this understanding that will draw out of us all the goodness and gift-edness with which each of us has been blessed by God.* [John Powell, *The Christian Vision*, p. 62]

Decision-Making Questions

Here are a couple of examples of some of the questions and issues other teens have struggled with in deciding how they felt about having sexual intercourse:

> *To me, you can't decide about intercourse until you decide about marriage. I don't necessarily mean whether you want to marry the person you're thinking about having sex with. What I mean is how you feel about marriage. Do you want sex to be something you only do with that one special person in your life? I feel down on marriage in a lot of ways because my parents got divorced when my dad was messing around with this real estate agent. But if you're going to be married, I think there needs to be something to make it special. I may date a dozen people before I get married. If I have sex with every single one of them, what's left to be special about marriage?*

> *I explained all this to the guy I'm dating now, and I think he understands. He'd like to go ahead and have sex now, but I'm not willing. I like him even more because he respects that even though he doesn't agree. I never feel any pressure from him.* Female–Evangelical Lutheran Church

> *I have trouble deciding what to wear to school every day. My mother finally made me start to lay my clothes out the night before! And I have this big need to talk about everything. I know that I make my boyfriend crazy talking about whether to have sex. He's more like, Okay, let's do it*

or not do it, but don't talk about it anymore because I can't take it. But I think it's so important to be sure it means the same thing to both people. And you have to be sure it's all right with God.

What does the Bible really say about it? I know it talks about fornication, but is that really sex before marriage? It's not like people dated and went to the movies or anything back then. I think I drive my Sunday school teacher crazy asking questions about this stuff, maybe because she doesn't know the answers. Female–United Methodist Church

Here are some questions for you to think about in terms of your own decision-making about sexual intercourse with a specific person. Space has been provided for you to insert some brief thoughts in this book, but you may also decide to do the writing in your mind or in a journal.

You may also decide to come back to these questions after you have read the chapters that follow. Those chapters have more to say about what other religious teens have done sexually and how they feel about it. You'll also find an overview of what the Bible says about sexuality.

Do you want to wait until you are married to have sexual intercourse? How do you feel about intercourse in terms of your relationship with God?

Do you want to wait until you are older and have had more dating experiences before having sexual intercourse? How do you think intercourse would affect you at this point in your life?

How do you feel about your communication with the other person? Have you share your beliefs and values about sexual activity? What else do you need to discuss before intercourse? Have you talked about the past sexual experience you have each had [not necessarily the names of the persons you've been with but what you've done]?

Have you made adequate arrangements for protection against pregnancy and sexually transmitted disease? If the protection did not work, do you know what you would do in response to a pregnancy or a sexually transmitted disease? Have the two of you talked about that?

What will sexual intercourse add to your relationship with the other person? Will it really offer anything that you can't have through other ways of expressing physical affection? How important is it to move to intercourse?

How will having sexual intercourse affect your relationship with God? Have you prayed about this decision?

Chapter Six
Masturbation, Kissing, And Touching

Masturbation is how I get pleasure, and it makes it easier not to go too far with a boy. I'll touch tongue with a guy I like but nothing more than that. No touching the breasts, and no taking clothes off.
                                        Female–Roman Catholic

Masturbation is one of the main ways that both males and females experience sexual pleasure. For many, like the girl in the opening quote, masturbation may make it easier not to go too far with other sexual experiences.

We all have a sexual response cycle that can be experienced through a variety of sexual activities. Masturbation, fondling of the breasts or the genitals by a partner, oral sex, anal sex, and sexual intercourse can all lead to essentially the same series of responses by our bodies:

1. Excitement, when a person first begins to be turned on or aroused.
2. Plateau, when a person's excitement increases even more and then holds at that level for a time [often a short time].
3. Orgasm, which is often referred to as "coming." This is the time of ejaculation for a male, and semen squirts from the penis. This is the time when a woman may feel a pleasurable sense of contractions and a sense of release.
4. Resolution, which is a pleasant sense of relaxation.

When people are feeling turned on, strongly aroused, their bodies are getting ready for sex. Both men and women, as they become aroused and begin to move through the response cycle, experience tense muscles, a more rapid heartbeat, faster breathing, flushed skin [sometimes a measles-like rash], and erect, more sensitive nipples and breasts. A man's penis becomes erect; a woman's clitoris enlarges and her vagina becomes wet. The woman's uterus moves higher, creating space for the penis. While these changes to the penis, clitoris, and vagina prepare the body for intercourse, the body can experience orgasm through other activities [like masturbation, oral sex, fondling by a partner, and anal sex].

Masturbation

Masturbation refers to giving yourself pleasure by touching and rubbing your genitals, often to the point of orgasm. Because masturbation has been thought by some as sinful, shameful, or even harmful, it may be more difficult for many of us to talk about and feel okay about than some other topics related to sexuality.

> Almost all people masturbate at some time
> in their lives, and most people pretend that
> they don't.

Some religious traditions teach that masturbation is wrong. There is no Biblical basis for that view. The belief that masturbation is wrong is grounded in the perspective that sexuality is expressed at its best and most fully in accordance with God's plan when that expression takes place between a man and a woman in the institution of marriage. Thus this perspective argues that masturbation as a solitary act does not represent the form of sexual expression that should be sought.

> *Some refer to Genesis 38:8–10 which talks about*
> *the sin of Onan. Onan was criticized, however,*
> *not for masturbation but for withdrawing his penis*
> *from Tamar before ejaculation. He was supposed*
> *to provide children for his brother's widow [see*
> *Deuteronomy 25:5–6]. In our time, we do NOT*
> *believe a man has an obligation to provide children*
> *for his brother's widow, but this Old Testament story*
> *reflects a different culture in which a harsh life meant*
> *that children were desperately needed. People who*
> *claim this passage is against masturbation do not*
> *understand the passage.*

When I visited with priests, ministers, rabbis, seminary professors, and officials in denominations in preparation for this book, I encountered almost no one who still believed that masturbation is a sin. That includes some people in denominations that have official statements saying that it is a sin. The reality is that because most people are uncomfortable discussing masturbation, there is a tendency for doctrinal statements to remain on church records without serious, informed debate.

I do not believe that masturbation is a sin. I think that it is a means of achieving sexual pleasure and release that has been given to us by God. Gaining sexual pleasure through activities with another person is a much more complicated process than masturbation. Activities like oral sex, anal sex, and sexual intercourse carry with them the danger of HIV and of other sexually transmitted diseases. There's also a very strong emotional component to sharing sexual activities with another person, and it's important to be ready for those experiences. Masturbation can be a good means of dealing with sexual tension for persons not yet ready for a sexual relationship with another person.

The majority of the teens in the *Faith Matters* study have masturbated. There are no significant differences among the major religious traditions with the exception of Muslim teens. Female Muslims were less likely than females in other traditions to practice masturbation. Male Muslims did not show different rates of masturbation than other teens in the study. Catholic, Lutheran, United Methodist, Presbyterian, Mennonite, Pentecostal, and other Christian teens all showed about the same percentage of masturbation, as did Jewish teens.

Percentage Who Masturbate

Males 9th-10th	Females 9th-10th	Males 11th-12th	Females 11th-12th
81.2%	60.8%	89.4%	71.3%%

Here are comments from some teens about masturbation:

> *Sometimes I worry about being addicted to masturbation.*
> *I do it almost every night. I don't have a girlfriend, and*
> *I know it would be wrong to have sex with her if I did*
> *have one. What I do for myself keeps me from being too*
> *frustrated, but I don't talk to anyone about doing it. You*

can talk with guys in my school about intercourse or oral sex or whatever, but no one owns up to what they do under the covers at night. Male–United Church of Christ

I've found some creative uses for the shower nozzle. It feels so good, no one knows what I'm doing, and then I just finish cleaning myself. Female–Mennonite Church

My church teaches that masturbation is wrong. But everything that I've read says that it's a normal thing that almost everybody does. There's nothing in the Bible that convinces me there's something wrong with giving yourself pleasure. Isn't it a lot better to do it with yourself than to have premarital intercourse? Male–Missouri Synod Lutheran Church

A few teens who helped in the development of this book asked a logical question: How is masturbation done? No one gives a teenager a manual on the topic! And boys sometimes wonder how girls do it, and girls wonder how boys do it. There are in fact many different ways to masturbate. Some people also fantasize about something [or someone!] when masturbating.

Boys often masturbate by holding and caressing their penis and testicles, usually in an up and down motion. Some boys prefer to lie on their stomach, move their hips up and down, and rub their penis against the bed or pillow.

Girls use various combinations of the following techniques: stroking the clitoris and the areas around it; moving an object or the fingers in and out of the vagina; or squeezing and releasing the muscles of the inner thighs and vagina. Many girls find that their own natural secretions provide enough lubrication to make masturbation pleasurable. Other girls use petroleum jelly or their own saliva for wetness.

Some girls enjoy rubbing their nipples as a build-up to masturbation. Boys are less likely to find rubbing their own nipples arousing, but some do.

There are some myths about masturbation:

Myth: *Masturbation is okay as long as you don't do it too often.* There is no evidence that masturbating frequently is harmful. There is really no such thing as "masturbating too much." Masturbation can have a negative impact if it causes a person to become withdrawn or if the frequency begins to interfere with homework, time with family or friends, or other important activities. For someone with anxiety about getting involved in a relationship, masturbation [or a hobby, job, television, or the Internet] can serve as a substitute for contact with other people. You don't need to worry about the frequency unless it starts to interfere with other activities or relationships. There is also nothing "wrong" with you if you choose not to masturbate.

Myth: *Masturbation is an immature form of sexuality–people with sex partners don't need to masturbate* Masturbation is something you can enjoy throughout life. Sometimes it is a way to release sexual tension when you are not involved in a sexual relationship. At other times you may masturbate just because it is a way of giving yourself pleasure. Masturbation is not just a substitute for "real sex." It is a different way of giving yourself pleasure.

Myth: *Masturbation will make you go blind, go crazy, become sterile, or grow hair on your palms.* No, no, no, and no. These old myths probably grew out of adults trying to scare kids out of touching their own bodies. It may have scared a lot of kids, but it probably didn't stop them from masturbating–they just checked their palms more often!

Take just a few moments to think about the topic of masturbation. Check each of the following statements if it is true in your experience. Since this is such an uncomfortable topic for so many, you may want to make the checkmarks in your head rather than in the book! [And you may wish to do the same with some of the other exercises in this book.]

___ I enjoy masturbating.
___ I can't tell from conversation whether my friends masturbate or not.
___ My friends make jokes [sometimes crude!] about masturbation, but they aren't about to have a serious conversation about it.
___ I feel some relief to know that so many other religious teens masturbate and that my faith leaders may not be against it.

71

___ I can ask my parents or another trusted adult my questions about masturbation.

Kissing, Touching, Being Naked

The majority of the teens in the *Faith Matters* study are not having premarital intercourse or oral sex. That doesn't mean they aren't having sexual contact with other people. Note the percentages who have been involved in petting [fondling the partner's breasts or genitals] and who have been completely nude with a member of the opposite sex [within the last two years, so that bathtub play as young children is not counted]:

Petting
(Fondling a partner's breasts and/or genitals)

Males 9th-10th	Females 9th-10th	Males 11th-12th	Females 11th-12th
28.8%	30.7%	71.6%	70.9%

Being completely nude with a member of the opposite sex

Males 9th-10th	Females 9th-10th	Males 11th-12th	Females 11th-12th
16.3%	17.6%	50.3%	47.2%

The percentages who have been involved in petting and who have been nude with a member of the opposite sex are much higher for 11th and 12th graders than for 9th and 10th graders. As teens go out more and have more opportunities for privacy, these behaviors increase.

Those statistics raise some obvious questions. Did we ask them to distinguish between fondling the breasts and fondling the genitals? No. We should have. Have those who have been completely nude with a member of the opposite sex all been involved in making out or petting? Yes, with the exception of six persons. Have all those who have had intercourse or oral sex been completely nude with a member of the opposite sex? No.

A few who have had intercourse and more who have had oral sex have done so without taking off all their clothes.

The written comments on the surveys, the interviews with selected teens, and the discussion of the survey results with some teens have pointed to another area of sexual activity which we didn't directly cover with a survey question and should have: what some teenagers call "dry humping." This happens when people have direct genital-to-genital contact without skin-to-skin contact in the process. They keep their clothes on and rub against each other, generally to the point of ejaculation for the boy. Because there is no exchange of fluids, the teens correctly see this as a way to avoid the risk of pregnancy or disease. Some of them also see it as an activity not clearly prohibited by Scripture or by faith community teaching.

There are variations on dry humping. Some do it wearing street clothes. Some do it on or near the beach wearing swimming suits. Some strip to their underwear. In some instances, the male will remove his underwear, but the female leaves her underwear on. [The boy taking off his underwear and the girl wearing only underwear makes it more likely that fluids might be exchanged.] There are some parts of the country where the phrase dry humping is used to describe the intimate contact in certain styles of dancing; but that contact, while highly arousing, does not usually lead to orgasm on the dance floor.

Some media stories have focused on the growing popularity of coed sleepovers [as opposed to the more traditional same-sex slumber party]. Our study did not include any direct questions about coed sleepovers, but we did have over two hundred youth who offered comments about coed sleepovers. About three-fourths of those commenting expressed resentment of adult suspicion of coed sleepovers and maintained that kids did not have sex at the sleepovers in which they participated. Nine percent of those commenting on the topic said they knew of people having sex at coed sleepovers. Youth, pastors, and adult youth advisors were quick to point out in focus groups that males and females generally sleep in separate areas at congregationally sponsored lock-ins. Lock-ins are overnight retreats held in the church or synagogue at which youth rest for part of the night in sleeping bags or simply stay up all night participating in a variety of discussions and activities.

73

And what about kissing? Yes, there's certainly plenty of that going on. Some teens, however, kiss their friends on the cheek even if not involved in any kind of dating or going out relationship. Thus it's important to be cautious in interpreting what teens say about kissing. Almost all the teens in the study have kissed a member of the opposite sex, but that doesn't always mean the same thing. The percentage of teens who have been involved in kissing that included the insertion of the tongue into the mouth of the other person ran about the same as for petting [around 30% for 9th and 10th graders and 70% for 11th and 12th graders].

We asked the youth in the study if they thought it was all right to kiss when going out with someone for the first or second time. Among 9th and 10th grade males, 96.2% said that it was; 93.8% of the females in those years of school said that it was. Among 11th and 12th grade males, 97.4% said that it was; 94.1% of the females that age said it was. Some females, however, offered the observation that males who did not make a move for a kiss on a first or second date made a very positive impression. They felt more respected by males who were not in a hurry to initiate that kind of contact. Here are a few of the comments the youth offered concerning touching, being nude with the opposite sex, and related experiences:

> *I like my neck being kissed. . . and his nibbling on my ear. Doing that and holding each other close feels so good. That's enough for me. I don't need more.*
> Female–United Church of Christ

> *Feeling up is the big thing with my boyfriend. He's a real breast man. If he did it more gently, I'd like it. But it does more for him than for me.* Female–Roman Catholic Church

> *We like to get naked and touch each other and be close. We've started rubbing each other all the way to the big O, and I love that. I don't see a need for us to do anything more.* Male–United Methodist Church

> *I love her so much, and it just seems natural to be naked together when we have the privacy to do it. We masturbate each other to orgasm, but we decided not to have intercourse or oral sex. Who wants to take a chance on AIDS?* Male–Synagogue

*We've done some pretty intense making out. At first
I loved it. But now we keep wanting to do more. We
want to be naked with each other and to have oral
sex. But I don't feel ready for that. We might have
been better off if we hadn't gone so far so fast.*
Female–Episcopal Church

The youth also had some interesting comments to share related
to arousal, which can of course come in a multitude of ways:

*When I watch some movies, like American Pie, which
I've seen like 20 times, I get horny. I really want to
do something by myself or with someone else.* Female–
Synagogue

*I wonder if I could be oversexed or something. I go
through the day getting turned on by so many different
things. By good looking girls, by good looking teachers,
by things I read, by movies. I have this English teacher
who is so hot. She's maybe 25 years old and looks like
Cameron Diaz. I'm not kidding. One day she walked by
my desk and put a hand on my shoulder for just a second
I got such a boner I didn't know if I would be able to leave
when the bell rang.* Male–Pentecostal Holiness Church

*My youth pastor gave me some great advice. He said
you'd be big as a house if you ate each time you felt
hungry and that you'd be exhausted if you had sex each
time you felt aroused. The arousal is normal, but it
doesn't mean you have to do something.* Male–
Presbyterian Church USA

*I thought I was abnormal until we had this good discus-
sion in Sunday school. You can get aroused by all kinds
of things. I knew that was true for me, but I never heard
anyone talk about it. I had read this article about girls not
getting aroused by as many things or as fast as guys.
But from what our Sunday school teacher and some
others in the class said, that isn't always true. I felt so
much better after the class. I was about to write that I
needed that more than Bible study, but we got into it
talking about David and Bathsheba.* Female–Evangelical
Lutheran Church

Take a few moments to think about what you've read about kissing, touching, and arousal. Put a checkmark [in the book or in your mind] for each of the following statements which is true for you:

___ I was surprised that so many people have fondled each other.

___ I was surprised that so many people have been nude with each other.

___ Dry humping is popular with people in my school.

___ I have been nude with a member of the opposite sex and enjoyed it.

___ I have engaged in fondling with a member of the opposite sex and enjoyed it.

___ I really don't feel ready for being nude with a member of the opposite sex.

___ I really don't feel ready for fondling with a member of the opposite sex.

___ I feel like I am too young for these experiences, but it's helpful to read about them.

Remember that what other people do and do not do sexually should not be what determines what *you* choose to do. It's helpful to know how others feel about the experiences they've had, but that doesn't mean you'll feel the same way. You can also tell from the examples you've read in this chapter that different people feel different ways about the same experiences.

Some girls are aroused by other girls; some boys are aroused by other boys; and some people are aroused by both males and females. I'll talk more about homosexuality and bisexuality in Chapter Eight.

You have to determine for yourself what sexual activities are acceptable to you at your point in life and whether or not you want to share in those activities with a particular person. Remember that it's always better to error on not doing something than on doing it. The kinds of intense fondling and being nude with another person described in this chapter are very intense experiences and can certainly lead to orgasm. You want to be absolutely ready for such experiences. Many teens in the *Faith Matters* study told me that they were sorry they had certain experiences so early; no one said that he or she was sorry for delaying a particular sexual experience.

Chapter Seven
Oral Sex and Intercourse

*It's clear to me that the church and my parents and my
school think sex before marriage is wrong. But no one
is all that clear about why it's wrong. I respect these
people, but this is a topic we are never able to talk about.*
Female–United Methodist Church

Some people will read this book straight through, beginning
on the first page and ending with the last. Others will skip
around, reading what seems of greatest concern or interest at a
particular time. Almost everyone will read this chapter. Few
topics are of greater interest than sexual intercourse and oral
sex, and few topics are as difficult for young people to gain
accurate information about from parents, congregations, and
schools.

You already know that almost all parents, teachers, clergy,
and other caring adults feel that most teenagers are not ready
for such intimate experiences as oral sex and premarital
intercourse. These same adults generally feel that these are
activities that should be reserved for people who are married.
You also know that, in spite of the attitude of adults toward teen
sex, large numbers of young people are choosing to have these
experiences.

My intention, not only in this chapter but in the book as a
whole, is to provide you with the needed information and
perspective to make healthy decisions for yourself. Decisions
about sexual intercourse and oral sex should not be made in
isolation from your overall understanding of sexuality, of
relationships with other people, of the Bible and your faith
tradition, and of the significant health decisions involved. Thus
if you've skipped ahead to this chapter, I hope you'll go back
and read the earlier chapters after you've read this one. And
read the chapters to come about the Bible, sexually transmitted
disease, contraception, abortion, marriage, parenting, and other
issues related to intimate sexual activity. I'll also seek along the
way to help you think about your decision-making process.

In this chapter, I'll share some factual information about
intercourse and oral sex. I'll also share some figures about what
young people in the *Faith Matters* study have actually done, and

I'll share how they've felt about the experiences they've had. I'll share some information about how teens view these matters from a religious perspective, and I'll raise some important questions for you to think about in terms of your own spiritual life and sexual choices.

Some Facts about Sexual Intercourse

What is sexual intercourse? A mechanical definition sounds simple enough: the insertion of a man's erect penis into a woman's vagina. That's what happens. But the matter is more complicated than that. At least most people think so. Try this quiz to see how accurate the information that you have about intercourse really is:

True or False?

_____ 1. A man and a woman can't have intercourse unless the man has at least a partial erection.

_____ 2. Knowing how to insert the penis into the vagina comes naturally to most people.

_____ 3. A woman doesn't have to be as aroused or sexually excited as a man before intercourse.

_____ 4. A woman takes longer than a man to be fully aroused.

_____ 5. Intercourse alone is more likely to result in orgasm for the man than for the woman.

_____ 6. Size isn't everything, but a small clitoris for a woman and a small penis for a man may make it harder to enjoy intercourse.

_____ 7. A man can lose an erection during intercourse.

_____ 8. After inserting his penis into the woman's vagina, a male can usually wait five to ten minutes before ejaculation.

Here are the answers:

1. **True.** Without an erection, it is difficult or impossible for a man to get his penis into a woman's vagina.

2. **False.** Satisfactory intercourse requires practice and good communication. No one "naturally knows" how or when to insert the penis. Sometimes the man guides the penis using his fingers. Sometimes the woman will guide the penis. The first few attempts at intercourse are awkward for most people. It just doesn't happen as smoothly as portrayed in the media.

3. **False.** Both the man and woman must be aroused in order for intercourse to be a good experience. Arousal [sexual excitement] causes the secretion of a moist liquid in the woman's vaginal area and makes it easier for the penis to be inserted. If a woman is not aroused sufficiently for the vaginal opening to be lubricated and ready to stretch enough to accommodate the penis, then intercourse may be painful for the woman.

4. **True.** Well, at least this is true much of the time. Some males can get sexually aroused just thinking about being touched. It takes a little longer for most females to feel sexually aroused, to have the vaginal area lubricated, and to feel ready for intercourse. Many couples find it wise for the man to give more stimulation to the woman than the woman to the man during initial foreplay [kissing and touching in preparation for intercourse].

5. **True.** Most men are able to experience an orgasm more easily than most women during penile-vaginal intercourse alone. Ejaculation and orgasm go together for the man. Most women need direct clitoral stimulation.

6. **False.** Size of the clitoris and size of the penis have virtually nothing to do with satisfaction from intercourse or from other sexual activity. The actual variation in clitoral size among women and in penis size among men is just not that great when people are sexually aroused. Size differences are more apparent when people are not aroused.

7. **True.** A man certainly may lose an erection during intercourse. No matter how experienced the couple, there are times when a man will lose an erection before either the man or the woman has experienced orgasm.

8. **True.** Most men ejaculate within five to ten minutes of the time that they enter the woman's vagina. With practice and effort, some men are able to wait longer.

CORONARY CARE ALERT! Some adults who are reading this book may be about to go into cardiac arrest because of the kind of explicit information about sexual intercourse just provided. The *Adult Guide* [which is available as a companion to this Book] gives a more detailed explanation of why I've chosen to include this information. But just in case you don't have the *Adult Guide*, here are the reasons: First, I am confident that providing the right information to teens does not make it more likely that they will have intercourse. If anything, it makes it less likely. Sexual intercourse is a complex interaction between two people, and the facts make that clear. Second, the *Faith Matters* study taught us that young people are searching for the answers to these kinds of questions on the Internet, in the media, and from their friends. But they aren't always getting accurate information. Isn't it better for them to receive the information from a religious perspective than from sources that do not care about their well being? Third, with the exception of young people who determine that they have an exclusively homosexual orientation, most of those reading this book will in time marry and be having sexual intercourse in that context. It seems appropriate to teach them the things that they need to know for that to be a good experience. Certainly one can argue that they don't need that information until they are engaged, but that attitude ignores the ease with which the wrong information is available and also reflects a lack of trust in young people to make good decisions. So if you are an adult reading these words, take a deep breath, say a prayer, and keep on reading.

Youth in the *Faith Matters* Study and Intercourse

The youth completing our surveys show lower rates of sexual intercourse than is reflected in most secular studies. The rates are lower for all the subgroups we have analyzed in the survey including Caucasian teens, African-American teens, Hispanic teens, evangelical teens, Catholic teens, mainline Protestant teens, Unitarian Universalist teens, Jewish teens, and Muslim teens. No particular religious traditions showed markedly lower rates of sexual intercourse than other religious traditions except for Jewish and Muslim youth, who were less likely to have had intercourse than Christian youth.

The study did, however, find a subcategory of teens who had rates of sexual intercourse which were not only lower than many secular studies have shown but which were also lower than for the other teens in this study. Those teens [1,093 or 18.8%] share these characteristics:

- They attend religious services one or more times a week.
- They pray daily.
- They have involvement in at least one congregational group besides religious education and worship.
- They say that the teachings of the congregation and/or the Scriptures have "a lot of influence" on their sexual decisions.
- They say the congregation has provided information on how to make sexual decisions and on what the Scriptures says about sexuality.
- They feel a strong connection with congregational leaders who work with youth.
- They feel a strong connection with other youth in the congregation.
- They feel the adults who work with them portray sex in a healthy and positive way.
- They say their congregation encourages abstinence from intercourse for high school aged people.

The encouragement of abstinence by the church, synagogue, or mosque is a factor, but it is only one factor in this group of youth who were especially unlikely to have had intercourse. Most of the factors are positive in nature: strong attendance and involvement in the faith community, strong connections with other youth and with adults who work with youth, and what they see as a healthy and positive view of sexuality on the part of adults who work with them.

That does not mean that the youth in this category feel that they are receiving all the information about sexuality that they need from their congregational experiences. These youth, like others who participated in the study, did not feel that they received the total range of information or guidance from the congregation that they needed in relation to sexuality, dating, marriage, and parenting. This book is an attempt to provide more of that information.

For youth sharing the characteristics identified above, the percentage who've had sexual intercourse follows:

	9th-10th Grades	11th-12th Grades
Male	6.3%	16.5%
Female	6.7%	15.8%

For youth NOT sharing all the characteristics identified above, the percentage who've had sexual intercourse:

	9th-10th Grades	11th-12th Grades
Male	14.4%	33.9%
Female	16.7%	31.6%

For all youth participating in the study [combining both the groups identified above], the percentage who've had sexual intercourse:

	9th-10th Grades	11th-12th Grades
Male	12.7%	30.9%
Female	14.7%	28.0%

The 2003 figures from the Youth Risk Behavior Surveillance System (YRBSS) of the National Centers for Disease Control and Prevention indicate a much higher percentage of students who have had sexual intercourse. Overall, 42.9% of teenage females and 48.5% of teenage males in the United States have had sexual intercourse according to the YRBSS figures. Those figures show that 34.4% of 9th graders and 60.5% of 12th graders have had intercourse.

While the percentages of all the youth in our study who have had intercourse are lower than in secular surveys, it is important to note that the sample size of 11th and 12th grade youth was not as large as the sample of 9th and 10th grade youth. It is possible that youth who drop out of congregational activity in the later years of high school may be more likely to have had sexual intercourse than those who stay. Many of the youth who are not having intercourse are nevertheless involved in other forms of sexual activity like fondling, being nude with each other, and having oral sex. Here are some of the comments from teens about sexual intercourse:

The first time was horrible. I wondered why anyone would want to do it. My boyfriend. . . just caused me pain. I'll give him credit. When he figured out that it hadn't been good for me, he felt really bad. Then he started working harder so it would be better for me. Now it feels good most of the time, and I like being that close. But I still don't think I've had an orgasm. . . . I don't understand some of my friends who have had sex with four or five different guys. Letting someone inside of you is such an intimate thing. I wouldn't want to do it with someone I didn't love. I do think sex is a gift from God, but I don't see waiting until marriage. Female–Roman Catholic Church

Guilt stops me. We probably shouldn't do everything that we do, but I draw the line at intercourse. You can't undo that. I don't know if I'll wait until marriage or not, but I'm not going to do it in high school. Female–Unitarian Universalist Church

Everyone makes too big a thing out of sex. It's fun. It's a way to be close. It doesn't require a lifetime commitment. The first couple of girls I did it with, did the whole enchilada, I made a mistake in not being clear. Now I let the girl know that this isn't a marriage proposal. It's sex. If she doesn't want to do it, that's fine. But don't be expecting an engagement ring. Male–Independent Christian Church

I don't think I've had an orgasm. The earth never shakes. I don't quiver and moan like my boyfriend does. Sometimes I wonder why I keep doing it. Am I afraid of losing him? Is it a habit now that I can't break? It doesn't do that much for me, and I get filled with guilt. Female–Independent Baptist

83

> *I don't know how to describe it, but it's wonderful. I feel wide awake and exhausted all at once. More awake than awake. More tired than tired. I don't see how there can be anything wrong with this. God made us this way.* Female–United Methodist Church
>
> *I'm not ready for intercourse. We've found a lot of ways to give pleasure to each other that don't involve the risk of pregnancy or disease. We like to dry hump. We get all the way to orgasm but keep our clothes on. Is that wrong?* Male–Missouri Synod Lutheran Church
>
> *I have so many friends who have messed up their lives by getting pregnant. Our youth pastor reminds us that there may be safer sex but there's no such thing as SAFE sex. I'll do a lot of things, but nobody is going to stick his d - - - in me before a wedding ceremony. Forget it. Jesus doesn't want it, and I don't want it.* Female–African Methodist Episcopal Church

Some Facts about Oral Sex

Oral sex refers to one person using his or her mouth on the genitals of the other person, giving pleasure through a combination of licking, sucking, and stroking. The fingers are often used to supplement the action of the lips, tongue, and mouth. Some people choose this way of giving pleasure as an alternative to intercourse, and some do it in addition to intercourse. Try this quiz to see how accurate the information that you have about oral sex really is:

True or False?

____ 1. You can't get pregnant from oral sex.

____ 2. You can't get HIV/AIDS or another sexually transmitted disease from oral sex.

____ 3. The Bible clearly says that oral sex is wrong even for married people.

____ 4. Oral sex is disgusting.

____ 5. If the woman doesn't swallow the man's semen when he ejaculates in her mouth, it will damage his pleasure from oral sex.

____ 6. You can't enjoy oral sex with a condom.

Here are the answers:

1. **True.** No one has ever gotten pregnant from oral sex alone.

2. **False. Big time false!** You definitely can get HIV/AIDS and other sexually transmitted diseases from oral sex. Many of the young people who are having oral sex are not aware of this fact, and that puts them at significant risk.

3. **False.** The Bible doesn't say anything specifically about oral sex. You won't find "oral sex" or any of the other terms for it [fellatio for a person giving oral sex to a man and cunnilingus for a person giving oral sex to a woman] in the Bible. Some people take the fact that the Bible doesn't talk about oral sex as evidence that it is prohibited, but we don't assume that other things not mentioned in the Bible are automatically prohibited.

4. **False.** Well, at least the statement is false for most people. The majority of people who try oral sex do not find it disgusting; in fact the substantial evidence is that they like it a great deal. It is true, however, that there are some persons who are very uncomfortable with the idea of oral sex; for those persons it may truly be disgusting. It's important in healthy sexual relationships never to do something that one or both persons feel uncomfortable about experiencing. If the idea sounds disgusting to you, you have every right to feel that way; just be careful not to feel badly toward people who feel differently about it.

5. **False.** The woman does not have to swallow a man's semen in order for him to have pleasure from oral sex. Although semen has almost no taste, the issue here is that HIV and other sexually transmitted diseases can be spread when people have oral sex without the use of a condom on the man and a dental dam or other barrier on the woman.

6. **False.** In fact a couple may enjoy oral sex more with a condom because then they do not have to be afraid of getting or giving HIV/AIDS or another sexually transmitted disease. A

condom on a man does not keep either party from enjoying oral sex but protects the person giving the oral sex. Women receiving oral sex should have a dental dam or other barrier for the protection of the person giving the oral sex [more about this later].

Youth in the *Faith Matters* Study and Oral Sex

The extent of sexual activity by the youth in our study is greater than reflected by the statistics for intercourse alone. Our study shows that youth who are active in congregations, while less likely than the general youth population to have had intercourse, are nevertheless participating in other sexual behaviors. An earlier chapter talked about fondling each other and being nude with each other. Oral sex is another kind of sexual activity that many people find very pleasurable. As we have shared the *Faith Matters* study results, many clergy and other parents have been particularly surprised by the numbers of youth who are having oral sex.

Until very recently, little research information has been published on teens and oral sex. When we were designing our own study, we were surprised by how few secular studies of teens had included questions on this topic. Our own information was some of the first to be released. Now there are secular studies indicating that from a third to half of teens may have had oral sex by the time they finish high school.

The figures for oral sex in our study are for that activity with a member of the other sex. Oral sex in the context of a homosexual relationship was not covered in the *Faith Matters* survey. The youth who are having oral sex are not always the same ones who have had intercourse. Some have had intercourse but not oral sex; some have had oral sex but not intercourse; and some have had both oral sex and intercourse:

Intercourse and Oral Sex

	Intercourse	Oral Sex	Intercourse and/or Oral Sex
9th-10th Males	12.7%	11.4%	17.3%
9th-10th Females	14.7%	13.6%	19.5%
11th-12th Males	30.9%	28.9%	38.7%
11th-12th Females	29.0%	26.4%	37.6%

In most instances, those who have given oral sex have also received oral sex. Males are slightly more likely than females to have received but not given oral sex. Females are somewhat more likely to have given oral sex but not to have received it. As you can see from the table above, combining those who have given or received oral sex with those who have had intercourse results in a considerably higher level of sexual activity than the figures for intercourse alone.

Many of the teens in the *Faith Matters* study saw oral sex as involving not only no danger of pregnancy but also little or no danger of HIV/AIDS or other sexually transmitted diseases. As shared earlier in this chapter, it is quite possible to get HIV/AIDS and other sexually transmitted diseases from oral sex. Unfortunately about 55% of those completing our study do not realize that. People who are going to have oral sex must use protection from sexually transmitted disease.

Some young people also make a distinction between intercourse and oral sex in terms of what they see the Scriptures and the congregation teaching. While they see premarital intercourse being prohibited by the teachings of their tradition, many of the teens feel that the Scriptures and tradition are silent on the matter of oral sex. Here are some of the their comments about oral sex:

We keep trying to do 69. It's hard. How can you focus on your partner when she's doing that to you? We think this is a safe thing to do. No chance of pregnancy and almost no chance of a disease. And the Bible says absolutely nothing about it. I don't think it's wrong. Male– Evangelical Covenant Church ["69" refers to a couple performing oral sex on each other at the same time, thus fitting together like a six and a nine.]

I like it when he does oral sex on me first. Then I'm wet and hot, and it's easier to take him inside me. We just did oral sex until I was able to get the pill. Now we do both. Female–Roman Catholic Church

I was at this party where they played modified spin-the-bottle. When you were "it," you gave oral sex to the first person of the opposite sex the bottle landed on. Then that person would give it a spin and give it to the next person of the opposite sex it landed on. I thought it was gross, but I did it because I wanted to be part of the group. Now I wonder if it was a sin. My friends don't think so, but I'm not sure. Female–Southern Baptist Church

> **WARNING:** Games like the one just described create a tremendous danger of sexually transmitted diseases being spread. They also put enormous pressure on people to share in the activity. From a Christian perspective, perhaps the worst aspect of this kind of game is that it causes people to have a very intimate sexual experience with someone they do not know well and have had no opportunity to talk about what is and is not acceptable. Don't take part in that kind of activity. If you have friends who are doing so, warn them of the danger of HIV/AIDS and other sexually transmitted diseases being spread as a result.

I love it when my girlfriend gives me head. It feels sooooo good. And I feel so close to her when she does it. I would like to do the same for her, but she doesn't want it. She'll dry hump, but she doesn't want to take her clothes off. Male–Church of God

I liked oral sex the first time my girlfriend gave it to me. Then I saw how she felt used and dominated. I won't ever push anyone else to do it. Her feeling awful made me feel awful. Male–Church of the Brethren

The guy I was going with pressured me into doing it, and I went along. Now I don't feel so good about it.

It's about as intimate as intercourse — you're putting the other person inside you, just in a different opening. I don't think Jesus wants us to be that casual about something so important. Female–Presbyterian

Are Premarital Intercourse and Oral Sex "Wrong"?

We asked youth to respond to some items concerning what they feel their faith community believes and what their Scriptures teach concerning intercourse and oral sex. The following are the statements and the percentage of youth in the study in agreement with each one:

Are Premarital Intercourse and Oral Sex "Wrong"?

92.8%   My faith community believes that premarital intercourse is wrong.

67.3%   The Scriptures of my faith teach that premarital intercourse is wrong.

54.1%   I personally believe that premarital intercourse is wrong.

65.4%   My faith community believes that oral sex before marriage is wrong.

34.7%   My faith community believes that oral sex is wrong even for people who are married.

18.9%   The Scriptures of my faith teach that oral sex before marriage is wrong.

28.7%   I personally believe that oral sex before marriage is wrong.

The teens in this study clearly see a significant difference between sexual intercourse and oral sex from the standpoint of the faith community, the Scriptures, and their own beliefs. The vast majority of the teens in the study believe that their faith community sees premarital intercourse as wrong, but the percentage who feel the Scriptures of their faith are clear on the issue is somewhat lower. Then the percentage who personally feel premarital intercourse is wrong drops to only a little more than half the respondents. That figure needs to be balanced by the fact that 92.5% indicated agreement with this statement:

> **Sexual intercourse should only happen between people who have a commitment to each other.**

Many of the teens are not ready to say that sexual intercourse is only all right in marriage, but there is nothing casual about the view of most of these teens toward intercourse.

Fifty-four percent of the teens personally believe that pre-marital intercourse is wrong. Only 7% of those who felt personally that it was wrong have had it. The personal conviction that intercourse before marriage is wrong appears to have a greater influence on behavior than simply perceiving that the faith community believes it is wrong.

Oral sex is another matter. The percentage who think that their faith community believes oral sex before marriage is wrong is considerably lower than the number who have that perception concerning their faith community's view of intercourse. Less than one in five of the teens in this study think that the Scriptures of their faith clearly prohibit oral sex before marriage. A large percentage of these congregationally active teens, 71.3%, are not convinced that oral sex before marriage is wrong.

Slightly over a third of the teens, 34.7%, think that their faith community views oral sex as wrong even for persons who are married. Those who belonged to religious traditions that might be described as fundamentalist or conservative were more likely than the other teens in the study to think that their faith community saw oral sex as wrong even in marriage. The teens themselves from those fundamentalist and conservative religious traditions, however, were not more likely to be personally convinced that oral sex is wrong.

As shared earlier, 55% of the teens agreed with this state-ment: "A person cannot get a sexually transmitted disease from unprotected oral sex." Thus we have many teens in this study who are not convinced there is anything wrong with having oral sex before marriage and who do not recognize that it is possible to get sexually transmitted diseases from that activity. That's alarming since unprotected oral sex can so readily result in sexually transmitted diseases.

Here are some of the comments of the teens concerning how they feel about premarital intercourse and oral sex from the perspective of faith community and scriptural teachings:

> *Our youth pastor keeps telling us that it's wrong to have premarital intercourse. But when you read the Scriptures, it isn't all that clear. People got married when they were fourteen and fifteen years old in Bible times, so premarital sex wasn't a concern.* Male–Missouri Synod Lutheran

> *My Sunday school teacher has had a lot of influence on me. She helped me understand how sex is part of God's plan and belongs only in marriage. I'm waiting and happy to be.* Female–Nazarene Church

> *We had a big True Love Waits campaign in my church and my school, but nobody mentioned oral sex until I asked about it. Then I got told that of course it was wrong but not why it was wrong. It won't make you pregnant, and you won't get AIDS. Why is it wrong? The Bible says nothing about it.* Female–American Baptist Church

> *I don't plan to get married until after law school. I just know that I won't be able to go that long without having sex. But I know I'm too young right now. I've only been driving a car for six months. And I wouldn't do it unless I loved the person.* Male–African Methodist Episcopal Church

> *When I think about the responsibility to God and to the person I love, I know that intercourse is a big step. My pastor is right–it belongs in marriage.* Male–United Methodist Church

> *I have the opinion that the faith should have a lot to say about my relationship with a guy. It's not just whether or not to have sex. What about honesty? What about communication? What about touching? What about respecting and being respected? No one*

*helps you with this. The Torah has all these confusing
teachings. Which parts really apply to life today?*
Female–Synagogue

*My priest rocks and is not negative on sex. He helped
me see how God intends marriage to be. I feel good
about myself, and I know I'm worth waiting for.*
Female–Roman Catholic Church

*I had sex with this guy because I thought we were in
love. I thought we were going to get married when we
were both out of college. It felt right to do it. Then I
found out that he was doing it with another girl all
the time he was doing it with me. I am such a loser.
I've lost something that I can never get back.*
Female–Missouri Synod Lutheran Church

*My pastor and my youth group advisor have taught
me to pray about the things that I do–before I do them.
When I pray about whether or not to have sex with
Tracy, I never get a clear signal that it's all right.
Does that mean she's not the person I'll marry? Does
that mean it would be a sin to have sex with her even
if we were going to get married later? I don't know
the answers to the questions, but I do know that it
would be wrong to have sex before I get some kind
of all clear from God.* Male–Christian Church (Disciples
of Christ)

The Decision to Have Intercourse or Oral Sex

As shared earlier, this book contains considerably more
information than just this chapter that relates to the decision to
have sexual intercourse or oral sex. I hope you'll read the entire
book, and we'll be talking more about decision-making as we go.
Because the decision to have sexual intercourse or oral sex is
such a major one, however, I want to raise a few points about
that decision.

**First, you don't want to ignore the reality that every
major faith tradition teaches that sexual intercourse is best
and most fulfilling within marriage.** Most traditions believe
that God's plan for our lives reserves sexual intercourse for
marriage. Certainly congregations have done a horrible job

explaining to teenagers why they feel that way. But remember that there are good reasons why the Christian, Jewish, and Muslim faith traditions are so unanimous in not recommending premarital intercourse. Those reasons include concern about unintended pregnancy, HIV, and sexually transmitted disease; but those are not the only reasons. Sexual intercourse at its best brings not only a physical intimacy but also a spiritual intimacy between two people. Most teenagers are not ready for that kind of intimacy.

Second, you want to remain aware that these are very intimate activities and should only be done with a person you trust and with whom you share a commitment. Very few of the teens in the *Faith Matters* study were at all casual about the decision to have intercourse. Some of them were a little casual about the decision to have oral sex, in part because they mistakenly thought they could not get a sexually transmitted disease from that activity. As you can tell from the comments of the teens, those who did decide too casually to have intercourse or oral sex generally ended up sorry they had done so. Don't let that happen to you.

Third, don't believe people who tell you that "everybody" has intercourse or that "everybody" has oral sex. As you can see from the statistics shared in this chapter, that just isn't true. We found in conversations with young people in the *Faith Matters* study that there are schools in which people talk like everyone has premarital intercourse or oral sex. There are also schools in which people like to claim that couples who go out three or four times in a row always have sexual intercourse. Those claims are not true. **The majority of teens who are active in their churches or synagogues have not had sexual intercourse or oral sex.** Do not believe people who tell you otherwise.

Fourth, remember there are some important differences between how some males and some females feel about sexual intercourse and oral sex. The females in the *Faith Matters* study were more likely than the males in the study to feel that sexual intercourse and oral sex belonged in marriage. Both younger and older males wanted sexual activity to increase earlier in the relationship than females of the same age. When one adds to this the reality that females often date older males, the differences in expectation become even more striking. A seventeen-year-old boy dating a fourteen-year-old girl is likely to

93

have very different expectations of what they do sexually than she is. That's one of the reasons parents are so uncomfortable about girls dating guys who are older.

Fifth, do not ignore the reality that sexual intercourse carries the possibility of pregnancy and of sexually transmitted disease and that oral sex carries the possibility of sexually transmitted disease. I'll talk more in future chapters about these realities and about how to have safer sex with protection against those things happening. It remains true, however, that the only way to be 100% safe on both pregnancy and sexually transmitted disease is to not have intercourse or oral sex. If you are going to have them, then it's imperative to take every possible precaution.

Sixth, you need to work through for yourself what you believe is the right thing to do concerning sexual intercourse, oral sex, and other forms of sexual intimacy. In doing that, you need to consider many different factors including the teaching of your faith community and your personal relationship with God. Don't let anyone push you into an activity for which you are not yet ready. The only way to be sure that won't happen is to be sure for yourself what you think is right for you.

Seventh, couples need to talk together, in advance, about what they think it is all right and not all right to do sexually. Decisions by couples should not be made in the middle of kissing and embracing! It's hard to set sexual limits when you are aroused. It is always a good idea to talk about and agree how far you are comfortable going before you start fooling around! **No one should ever be pushed into a sexual experience that he or she does not want.** This book has an entire chapter about unwanted sexual activity–precisely because it is such a major problem in our society. If either person feels that an activity is not all right, then that activity is not all right for the couple. Both persons need to agree that they are ready for a particular level of intimacy. Remember:

> **If a couple isn't ready to talk openly about**
> **a particular sexual activity, they are definitely**
> **not ready to experience that activity!**

Here are some questions to consider before making the decision to have sexual intercourse or oral sex:

94

Question One: Are you personally ready for scxual inter-course or oral sex? Be sure you have had enough experience expressing physical affection that you under-stand something of what will be involved.

Question Two: Is the other person ready for sexual intercourse or oral sex? Older males dating younger females need to give special consideration to this question.

Question Three: Have you and the other person talked about your sexual desires, preferences, and values? If you aren't comfortable communicating with each other about sex, then you aren't ready for intercourse.

Question Four: Will premarital intercourse lower the meaning of sexual intercourse within marriage for you or the other person? If either person has concern about this, take that as a negative vote. You cannot "undo" sexual inter-course.

Question Five: Do you have the same level of commitment to each other? Spell it out. If one of you is thinking about marriage and the other is not, then that is a potential problem.

Question Six: Do both you and the other person feel that this is the morally right thing to do? Again, if either has concern, take that as a negative vote.

Question Seven: Have you advanced far enough in your level of physical intimacy that you are ready for sexual intercourse or oral sex? As you can tell from the comments of young people who have had intercourse and oral sex, the experiences can be uncomfortable and unpleasant. Fondling each other to orgasm can be more satisfying for some couples and does not require as much sexual skill or experience.

Question Eight: Do both persons really feel that sexual intercourse or oral sex offers intimacy and satisfaction that cannot be achieved by some other form of sexual activity? Most persons can experience an orgasm more easily with other forms of sexual activity.

Question Nine: Have you made adequate arrangements to avoid an unwanted child and to lessen the risk of sexually transmitted disease? For Roman Catholic young people, this involves the additional issue of how one feels about birth control relative to the teachings of the Catholic Church.

What if. . . .

You have had sexual intercourse or oral sex but now wish you had not? The Bible is clear about God's love for us and God's forgiveness for us. If you have had sexual intercourse or oral sex and have since begun to feel that doing so was wrong, share that with God in prayer. Be assured that God will forgive you and help you. Here's what a male in a Southern Baptist Church said:

> *Monica and I had sexual intercourse several times. It didn't go well the first couple of times, but we got better at it. We'd convinced ourselves it was okay to go ahead and do it because we thought for sure we'd get married. Then we broke up and didn't even want to talk to each other any more. . . . Then I thought, my God, what did we do? And you can't change it. . . . And we never did have the right information. At least my older brother convinced me to use a rubber. Otherwise, I hate to think about what might have happened. . . . I guess God will forgive us, but it's tough to feel this way.*

Your partner wants to have sexual intercourse or oral sex but you do not? Then say so with kindness but firmness. *No one* should have to take part in any sexual experience that he or she does not want. If your partner genuinely cares about you, then he or she will respect your wishes. If your partner does not care enough about you to respect what you want, then you are better off developing a new relationship anyway. Remember what a female in the Evangelical Lutheran Church said:

> *To me, you can't decide about intercourse until you decide about marriage. I don't necessarily mean whether you want to marry the person you're thinking about having sex with. What I mean is how you feel about marriage. Do you want sex to be something you only do with that one special person in your life? I feel down on marriage in a lot of ways because my parents got divorced when my dad was messing*

around with this real estate agent. But if you're going to be married, I think there needs to be something to make it special. . . . I explained all this to the guy I'm dating now, and I think he understands. He'd like to go ahead and have sex now, but I'm not willing. I like him even more because he respects that even though he doesn't agree. I never feel any pressure from him.

Your partner does not want to have sexual intercourse or oral sex but you do? Then the reverse applies. You should *not* force your desires on another person, and you should not try to talk your partner into an activity he or she does not want.

You and your partner really do not want to have sexual intercourse or oral sex yet but are finding it increasingly frustrating to resist doing so? Note the information in this book about kissing and fondling. There are many alternatives to sexual intercourse or oral sex in terms of satisfying the physical desires of each other.

You and your partner are interested in anal intercourse? The *Faith Matters* study did not include questions about anal intercourse, though some teens commented on it in response to other questions. The insertion of the penis into the anal opening happens both in homosexual relationships [between two males] and in heterosexual relationships. Some heterosexual teens have experimented with it because they see it as a way of being intimate but avoiding pregnancy. Anal intercourse exposes the couple to the same dangers of HIV/AIDS and other sexually transmitted diseases as oral sex or vaginal intercourse. It's essential to use a condom. Because feces come out the anus, there are dangers of infection that make hygiene very important. Insertion of the penis into the anal opening must be done with considerable care, since that opening does not have the flexibility of the vagina. Anal intercourse is a very intimate activity. Some people like it; some do not. Many people who have been married for years have chosen not to try anal intercourse because the idea is not appealing to them.

You and your partner both feel that sexual intercourse or oral sex is all right and want to experience it? Be sure that you have really thought through the issues involved and are both making this as a free and responsible decision. Be certain you have thought about how these acts relate to your faith. Remember that sexual intercourse, from the perspective of almost all denominations, is at its best in the relationship of marriage.

You should consider talking with your parents and other trusted adults before deciding to have sexual intercourse or oral sex. These are highly intimate activities, and they can change the direction of your life–especially if you participate in them without protection against pregnancy and disease. If your parents or someone in your church or synagogue gave you this book, you can feel pretty confident that you can approach that person or persons with your questions and concerns.

Sexual intercourse, from a religious perspective, is not just a physical act. There is a sense in which the souls or the spirits or the deeper selves of the man and woman unite during sexual intercourse. This is part of the reason that people find sexual intercourse so wonderful. It is also an experience which changes the lives of the individuals who experience it and also changes the nature of their relationship with each other. C.S. Lewis expresses it this way in a passage in his book *The Screwtape Letters*:

> The truth is that whenever a man lies with a woman,
> whether they like it or not, a transcendental relation
> is set up between them which is eternally enjoyed or
> eternally endured.

In 1 Corinthians, Paul refers to the body as the "temple of God." Thus what we do with our bodies is a matter of spiritual concern. Many forces in our culture lead us to believe that sexual intercourse and oral sex are casual activities. In many parts of North America, teens use the words "hooking up" and "friends with benefits" to refer to relationships with casual sex. But for many reasons already shared in this book, casual sexual relationships are not a viable option for a religious person.

Chapter Eight
Homosexuality and Bisexuality

I have this wonderful friend who's gay, but he
stays way in the closet at church. People in
our church are so disapproving of gays and
keep talking about the "gay agenda" for the
country. This guy doesn't have any agenda
except wanting to live his life and wanting to
be accepted. Why can't we do that in the church?
Female–Missouri Synod Lutheran

Not all people have the same sexual orientation. The American Psychological Association says that sexual orientation is "an enduring emotional, romantic, sexual, or affectional attraction to another person. . . . sexual orientation exists along a continuum that ranges from exclusive homosexuality to exclusive heterosexuality and includes various forms of bisexuality." Persons of homosexual orientation have a primary sexual attraction to the same sex in contrast to persons of heterosexual orientation who have a primary sexual attraction to the opposite sex. Bisexual persons are sexually attracted to both the same sex and the opposite sex. While their situation is not as well known, some persons are described as trans-gendered because they are biologically male or female but identify their gender as the other. This chapter will talk primarily about homosexuality but will also speak some about bisexuality and persons who are transgendered.

Some teenagers reading these pages would describe them-selves as having a homosexual rather than a heterosexual orientation. Most teens reading these pages know people their age who have a homosexual orientation.

Homosexuality and bisexuality are topics of considerable controversy in many congregations today. The words above from the Missouri Synod Lutheran teenager reflect the tension that young people in many denominations feel. My assumption is that there are persons reading this chapter who feel that homosexuality is a sin. There are others reading this chapter who feel that homosexuality is a part of God's design and should be affirmed just as much as heterosexuality. There are still others who are uncertain how to view homosexuality.

Before reading further in this chapter, take a few moments to think about your own sexual orientation, your view of homosexuality, and your perceptions of how homosexuality is viewed in Scripture and in your congregation. As with some other exercises in this book, you may want to place the yes or no responses in your mind rather than on the page if you are concerned about others seeing the book.

Yes or No?

_____ 1. I am clear about my own sexual orientation.

_____ 2. I have friends who are homosexual or bisexual.

_____ 3. A gay, lesbian, or bisexual person can find welcome and acceptance in my congregation.

_____ 4. A gay, lesbian, or bisexual person can be open about his or her orientation in my youth group.

_____ 5. My congregation teaches that homosexuality is a sin.

_____ 6. I think Scripture clearly states that homosexuality is a sin.

_____ 7. I think Scripture teaches us that love is always sacred.

_____ 8. I think Scripture affirms the goodness of creation and that all people are the children of God, regardless of their sexual orientation.

_____ 9. I don't think that people choose a particular sexual orientation. They just "are" what they are.

_____10. I think that gay and lesbian people should have the same legal rights as heterosexual people.

_____11. I think that gay and lesbian people should be able to get married if they want to do so.

_____12. I don't think I understand what it means for a person
to be transgendered.

Results of the *Faith Matters* Study

When we did the *Faith Matters* study, I thought that we
would find a smaller percentage of homosexual teenagers who
are involved in congregations than studies have found which
looked at North American society as a whole. My assumption
was that teens of homosexual or bisexual orientation would be
somewhat less likely to be involved in congregations, given the
number of religious traditions with a negative view of
homosexuality.

In looking at the results, it's important to be aware that
forming a sexual identity or orientation is something that
happens during the adolescent years.   Some sexuality
researchers report that as many as 25% of twelve year olds are
unsure of their sexual orientation but that only 5% of eighteen
year olds have that same uncertainty. People may be unclear at
the start of adolescence about their sexual orientation, but they
are usually not unclear by the end of that developmental time.

What the *Faith Matters* study found, in fact, was that a
surprisingly high number of teenagers who are involved in
congregations self-identified as homosexual or bisexual. In fact
some secular studies have reported lower percentages of teens
with homosexual or bisexual orientation than we found. As we
have shared the results with clergy and other congregational
leaders, most have been surprised by the percentage of teens
who didn't have a heterosexual orientation. These figures reflect
self-identification of orientation, not behavior. The fact that a
person feels he or she has a homosexual orientation does not
necessarily mean that person has actually participated in a
homosexual act.

	Males	Females
Heterosexual	86%	89%
Homosexual	7%	5%
Bisexual	5%	4%
Don't know	2%	2%

Some of the longest written comments in the study came
from youth who self-identify as homosexual or bisexual and who

have anxiety both about how to relate their sexual orientation to their faith and about how accepted they would be if their sexual orientation were known by the congregation. For example:

I'm about as deep in the closet as a homosexual can be. My parents don't know. No one in my youth group knows. Almost no one at school knows. This other guy and I have been good friends since second grade. When we were in the fifth grade, we started touching each other. Then we started to do other things and liked it. . . . Neither one of us is all that attracted to girls. We're careful not to hang out with each other too much at school. And fortunately our parents don't think anything about our spending time together in our rooms because we've always been friends. . . . Both of us are thinking we should ask girls to the prom. It isn't exactly fair to them in one way, but we'd probably be asking people who wouldn't get to go if not with us. . . . Kids at church and our youth advisor make these jokes about fags and queers. I'd never be accepted there if they knew I was gay. Junior– Southern Baptist Church

The only person in my synagogue who knows I'm bisexual is the girl that started doing things with me. . . . I think our rabbi believes that Jewish people are never homosexual–that it's like a condition that only Gentiles can get. . . . I just took for granted that I was a heterosexual when I was in middle school and a freshman. I dated and made out, and I loved doing that. . . . Then this friend and I were staying overnight, and we started talking about how the guys we dated didn't know how to touch you right. And we started doing things to each other, and it was great. I still like guys too, but it isn't possible for me to have as much pleasure with a guy as with her. . . . I think that many people have a homosexual side to them, but they bury it because society disapproves. . . . I can't decide whether God cares about my being bi. Senior– Synagogue

Secret Lives

The majority of the homosexual and bisexual teens in the study have not been open with clergy or other adult leaders in the congregation about their sexual orientation. Eighty-eight percent of the teens who self-identified as homosexual or bisexual indicated that their pastor or rabbi was not aware of their orientation. Only 36% indicated that there was a youth worker, advisor, or other adult leader [besides a parent] in the church who was aware of their orientation.

Eighty-three percent indicated that there was at least one other young person in the congregation who was aware of their orientation, so they are not completely isolated; but only 16% said that the whole youth group or class knew about it. Very few of them have felt sufficiently comfortable to "come out" to their entire youth group or class.

Almost half of these youth [46%] said that their parents were not aware of their sexual orientation or of their struggle over identifying their sexual orientation. I was deeply concerned as I went through survey responses and interviewed teens of homosexual or bisexual orientation to discover how many of them are leading secret lives–at least in their homes and in their congregations. Sexual orientation is a basic part of our identity, and it is a significant problem when teens are not able to comfortably talk about such concerns with their parents and in their youth groups or classes.

Non-heterosexual teens in our study were almost twice as likely as heterosexual teens to have seriously considered suicide. This should be a matter of great concern for those of us in congregations.

If the homosexual or bisexual teens felt that their pastor or another adult in the church was "open, accepting, or nonjudgmental" about matters of sexual orientation, they were much more likely to have talked with someone in the congregation about the topic. Here are some comments about adult leaders and congregational youth groups from teens with a homosexual, bisexual, or undetermined sexual orientation:

We have a great youth pastor. He always says that we can talk to him about anything, and he means it. I started talking to him last year because I was starting to realize that I was gay and didn't know what to do about it. Some friends at school already suspected that I was gay and were starting to make comments. . . . He was completely accepting. He told me that he felt like homosexual behavior was a sin but that he didn't think you could choose whether or not you had homosexual feelings. . . . He's kept talking with me and has struggled to understand what I'm going through. I

103

think some of his own opinions have been changed through talking to me. He gave me the courage to talk to my parents about this, and then he encouraged them to be supportive of me. I don't know what I would have done without him. Junior–Independent Christian Church

There is no way I can be open in my church about being lesbian. Our pastor has preached sermons on the sin of homosexuality and on the danger of having homosexuals as teachers in school and in any kind of church leadership. The others in the youth group say nasty things about the kids at school they think are gay. I just keep my mouth shut. . . . I don't want to be lesbian. That's just the way I am. God had something to do with this, and I don't think God feels the same way the church does. Sophomore–Nazarene Church

My minister is a strong advocate of rights for gay and lesbian people. He doesn't think being gay is a sin, and he's very open. . . . I talked with him a year ago when I was trying to figure out whether I was heterosexual or homosexual. . . . Then just a few weeks ago, I kind of came out to the youth group. I say kind of came out because it turns out that at least half of them already thought I was probably gay. The whole group was very supportive to me, and it was like a gigantic relief to not be hiding part of myself from them. I wish that kids at school would be as accepting. Sophomore–United Church of Christ

My father came out as gay about five years ago. My mother and my grandparents were terrified that I'd become gay because he was–like I could catch it like the flu. I think that I may be gay. Maybe it is in the genes. I don't know. I'm afraid to come out because it would cause all this trouble for my father. Male–Synagogue

I've talked with my pastor about my being gay, and he's done his best to help me. He doesn't think being gay is this big sin, but he also says that life is sure a lot easier if you're heterosexual. He's encouraged me not to be in a hurry to call myself gay. . . . The thing is, I just think I am gay. I can't do anything about it. Anyway, he's really kind even though he hopes I don't "stay" like this. Freshman–United Methodist Church

My pastor helped my parents get me in this program that is supposed to make you into a heterosexual. I was in this small group with four others from different churches. We kept getting yelled at and prayed for and made to sign commitment cards about not doing any homosexual acts. At first I resented it. Then I thought that maybe they were right. I mean, gay isn't normal. That isn't what most people are. But I still find myself attracted to other guys rather than to girls. What am I supposed to do? I hate being this way. I know the pastor and my parents and the drill sergeant guy all want to help me, but I don't think they understand. I'm trying to figure out for myself if God understands. Junior– Independent Christian Church

The *Faith Matters* study had many written comments from young people who see themselves as gay, lesbian, bisexual, or uncertain. I also interviewed many youth who were open about having a non-heterosexual orientation. It's very clear to me that almost none of the teens in the study who see themselves as homosexual or bisexual are "choosing" that orientation. Many of them readily acknowledge that it would be easier to be heterosexual and that they would like to be heterosexual because that is more accepted. Yet they find themselves with a non-heterosexual orientation or struggling with orientation issues.

Those youth who are non-heterosexual and who have a clergy person, youth group advisor, or youth group who are open and nonjudgmental are far more likely to be open within the congregation about their orientation. Those who were able to be open in their congregation were also less likely to have considered suicide than other non-heterosexual teens in this study. Those who are in congregations where there are negative views toward homosexuality and bisexuality rarely are open about their orientation. Those teens live with a very painful silence. A pastor in a United Methodist Church shared an interesting perspective:

Think about what it says that there are so many kids in our churches who are gay and who aren't open about it. If I were gay and felt disapproval from the church, I'd stop coming. But most of these young people are continuing

to be active. That says to me that God and the church are very important to them.

Is Homosexuality a Sin?

There are substantial numbers of persons in North America who see themselves as homosexual or bisexual in their orientation. As I shared in the previous section, it was clear to me from reading the comments of teens and from interviewing teens with a non-heterosexual orientation that they are not *choosing* that orientation.

Are all those persons guilty of sin? I find that hard to believe. Research on sexual orientation has not given us a firm answer on what causes a person to be homosexual or heterosexual or bisexual. Some scientists believe that people have a particular orientation that is theirs from the beginning. Others believe that people develop that orientation in ways we do not yet fully understand but that may include a combination of genetics, prenatal influences, environment, and experiences. It does appear part of God's design that some persons have a non-heterosexual orientation. With the creation story in Genesis and other passages of Scripture affirming the goodness of creation, I find it difficult to condemn homosexuality.

But how does a person reconcile an accepting attitude toward homosexuality with some of the biblical passages that seem to say that homosexual behavior is a sin? If you read some of those passages without considering the context, it does appear that Scripture says homosexuality is a sin.

There was no concept of homosexuality in biblical times as we understand it today. These were condemnations of sexual behavior between men, perhaps in reaction to the use of men and women as sacred prostitutes in nearby religious cults. Let's take a closer look.

First, let's consider the context of the passages most often quoted to show that homosexuality is a sin:

Genesis 19:1-11 really is an account of abuse and assault rather than an attack on homosexuality.

Leviticus 18:22; **Leviticus 20:13**; and **Deuteronomy 23:17-18** are part of what was called the "purity code" in Old Testament times. That same code also prohibits sex with a woman who is menstruating. Other passages in these Old Testament books require styles of dress that we no longer follow. People are also told to stone disobedient children! We do not, fortunately, put equal weight on every instruction found in Leviticus and Deuteronomy. Thus we should not automatically assume that the prohibition of same sex behaviors given here should be applied to life today.

1 Corinthians 6:9 has an uncertain meaning, and it depends on the translation used. The New International Version translates a word as "homosexual" that the New Revised Standard Version translates as "male prostitutes."

Romans 1:26-27 seems one of the clearest New Testament prohibitions on homosexual behavior. Some biblical scholars, however, have pointed out that Paul is not speaking here about those born with a homosexual orientation. He seems to be speaking about persons who are heterosexual but are acting as homosexuals–against their own orientation.

1 Timothy 1:10-11 may well have been condemning not homosexuality but pederasty, according to many biblical scholars. Pederasty was the practice of male teachers exploiting their position with male students by requiring them to have sexual relations with them. Thus these were not consensual acts and involved adults with children. In our own time, we would condemn such acts whether they were homosexual or heterosexual.

Second, with all of the passages just identified, it's important to remember that life was very short in biblical times. People were married at a very young age and had as many children as possible. Mary may have been as young as fifteen or sixteen when she gave birth to Jesus. With many people not living far into their thirties, family size was very important. In that kind of culture, it's understandable that homosexual behavior would have been discouraged.

The fact that it may have been discouraged does not necessarily mean that it is a sin. There are biblical passages that urge celibacy [not having sex at all], prohibit divorce, or expect women to be subservient to men. We do not consider those passages authoritative today. Why should we give strong weight to the very small number of passages that talk about homosexual behavior, especially given the context of those passages?

This seems especially true since Jesus doesn't mention same sex behavior in the gospels at all. Jesus never felt a need to reference homosexual behavior or to prohibit it. If it were a sin, why is Jesus silent on the topic?

Third, the Bible talks about the friendship of David and Jonathan, and some feel this could have been a homosexual relationship, especially because of 1 Samuel 18:1. There is a Hebrew word that can be translated as 'to gird, join, bind, or cling," which could imply a homosexual connection between them. 1 Samuel 20:41 talks about their kissing each other, but that action does not itself make a homosexual relationship. The truth is that we simply do not know with certainty what the passages mean. It is certainly true that the Old Testament celebrates the strong friendship that David and Jonathan had.

Fourth, while there are a small number of passages that are taken by some as condemning homosexual behavior, there are a much larger number of passages which urge us to:

- Show love and acceptance of others in all our relationships.

- Work for justice for all people and care about those who are looked down on by others. Jesus reached out to the poor, to the hated tax collectors, to prostitutes, and to others not cared about by society.

- Forgive persons who behave in ways that are not acceptable. Condemnation is never the last word with God. Jesus urges us in fact not to focus so much on the misbeheavior of others as on our own sins and shortcomings. For example, consider the passage in which Jesus tells people not to be focused on the speck or splinter in someone else's eye but on the log in their own [Matthew 7:1–5].

One of the best known teachings of Jesus is often called the Golden Rule and is part of the Great Commandment:

> **You shall love the Lord your God with all your heart and with all your soul, and with all your mind; and your neighbor as yourself.**
> **Luke 10:27**

Then Jesus proceeds to define who our neighbors are by telling the parable of the Good Samaritan, which in fact reminds us that all people are our neighbors [see Luke 10:25–37 for the full parable].

No one has any doubt that this is a commandment that applies to all of our lives. Those of us with a heterosexual orientation should ask ourselves how we would want to be treated if we had a homosexual orientation. We would want to be accepted and affirmed, as it seems clear to me Jesus would have done. Tony Campolo, a very respected evangelical leader, says this:

> *I believe that if Jesus were in our shoes, he would reach out in love to his homosexual brothers and sisters and demand that they be treated justly, that we end the discrimination that has too often made homosexuals into second-class citizens and denied them their constitutional rights.*
> [*Adventures in Missing the Point* by Tony Campolo and Brian McLaren; Emergent YS Books/Zondervan, El Cajon, 2003, p. 178]

The Congregation Is Important

The *Faith Matters* study found no differences between heterosexual and non-heterosexual teens in the importance they placed on religion in their lives, on their commitment to God, on their frequency of prayer, or on their commitment to the church or synagogue. The extensive written comments from nonheterosexual teenagers did make clear, however, that many of them struggle with their sexual orientation in relationship to their faith. For example:

> *I am so thankful that my pastor and church are not down on gay and lesbian people. My youth pastor sees being gay as another example of the diversity in people. I feel*

*like everyone in the church is very accepting of me. But
I feel sorry for some of my gay friends who are in churches
that do not feel that way. I couldn't keep going to church
if everyone disapproved of me.* Male–United Church of
Christ

*I can't be open with my parents or my church about being
gay. They see being homosexual as sinful. . . . . I don't
agree with them. I don't think that's how God sees me.
God made me this way, and I don't think it was a mistake.*
Female–Southern Baptist Church

*For a long time, I accepted what my church teaches. It's
not your fault if you have homosexual desires, but it is your
fault if you act on them. I'm not so sure that's right now.
Would God give you the desire, the feelings, if it was
wrong to act on them? Heterosexual people act on them.
I know I'm not ready for sex yet, but I will be in time. The
possibility of sex with a man has no appeal to me at all.
I'm not so sure that homosexual behavior is a sin.* Female–
Roman Catholic Church

*My rabbi thinks that homosexuality is wrong, but he has
a daughter who is a lesbian. At least that's what people
say. He does say that God loves homosexuals as much
as heterosexuals and that it's wrong for society to
discriminate against gays and lesbians. I'm convinced
that God loves me the way I am, and the way I am is
lesbian. I can't change it.* Female–Synagogue

Many of these teens are aware of religious teachings
that homosexual behavior is a sin but are not in
agreement with those teachings. The resulting
internal struggle is a difficult one for those teens
to whom involvement in their faith-based institutions
is very important.

The United Church of Christ, the Unitarian Universalists,
and the Reform Jews have official positions of acceptance of
homosexual people. Many religious traditions are unclear
about their positions on homosexuality. Teens in those
traditions pick up on that uncertainty:

*My church is confused. It's okay to be homosexual and
be a member of the church. But you can't be homosexual*

*and be a minister. Why is that? I do not understand.
I don't want to be a minister, so I should see it as a non-
issue for me.* Male–Presbyterian Church U.S.A.

*My father is the minister of our church. He goes to Annual
Conference every year, and every year there's debate
about something having to do with homosexuality. Dad has
changed his views on this since I worked up the nerve to
tell him that I was probably bisexual or a lesbian. He's
bought books about the Bible and theology that explain the
context of what the Bible says about sexual orientation.
Our denomination doesn't know what it believes on this
topic. You aren't supposed to be gay and be a minister,
but Dad knows several clergy who are gay. They just
don't announce it, and the bishop overlooks it. Dad says
most clergy would have a more accepting view if they
weren't afraid of losing financial support from conservatives
in the church.* Female–United Methodist Church

Whatever the official position of the church on homosexual
orientation and behavior, it is extremely important to remain
aware of the teens in local congregations who do feel they have a
non-heterosexual orientation and for whom the congregation is
extremely important. Those of us who are heterosexual have an
obligation to be concerned about the spiritual well-being and the
congregational acceptance of those who are homosexual.

Knowing People Who Are Gay

Ninety-six percent of the teens who completed surveys for
this study indicate that they know at least one person their age
[or within two years of their age] who has a gay, lesbian, or
bisexual orientation. Most know several such persons. The 4%
who indicated that they do not tended to be in more rural areas.
As shared earlier, many teens who have such an orientation are
reluctant to share that in their congregation much further than
with one or two especially close friends. But almost all teens
know someone their age who is gay, lesbian, or bisexual. This is
a part of life for teenagers today, and it is a part of life that congregations need to recognize.

We did not ask teens on the survey if they were open at
school about being gay, lesbian, or bisexual. Based on the

written comments of teens on the survey and on our interviews with teens, it appears to me:

- That religious teens are somewhat more likely to be open about a non-heterosexual orientation with more people at school than in the congregation.

- That there are some schools in which it is acceptable for non-heterosexual teens to be open about their orientation, and there are some schools in which it is very unacceptable.

- That even in the most accepting school settings, teens who are open about a gay, lesbian, or bisexual orientation can become the objects of ridicule, resentment, and insults. They can also become the targets of violence.

We had extensive written comments from gay, lesbian, and bisexual teens on the dangers of being open about their orientation at school. While some of them choose to do so, the price can be very high. Some heterosexual teens in the study shared insights about justice and homosexuality:

My friend Beth is lesbian. I'd known that she was for maybe a year before she worked up the courage to tell me. It's fine with me that she is. But as she's started to be more open about it, life has gotten harder for her. I'm deeply offended by the comments and disgusting jokes that are made at school about gay and lesbian people. . . . Our pastor talked in a sermon about the importance of standing up for what you think is right. That made me realize that I need to take a clearer stand for the rights of people like Beth. I shouldn't just keep my mouth shut when people make ugly comments. Christ would have come to the defense of people being treated that way. Female–United Methodist Church

The Golden Rule tells us to do unto others like we would want them to be to us. But that's not what happens in our relationships with gay people at school. Some of my friends from church think there's nothing wrong with putting down the f - - -. I don't think Jesus would see it that way. African-Americans like me have to deal with racism all the time. That should make us more sensitive to what gay people contend with. We should be champ-

*ions for others who are oppressed rather than part
of the oppression.* Female–National Baptist Church

Some of the teens who participated in the study have a
parent who is involved in a homosexual relationship. While
some of the teens with a parent who is openly gay feel
awkwardness and a little embarrassment about it, most said
that they have come to accept the orientation. Here are some of
the comments:

*My parents got divorced four years ago because my mother
came out as a lesbian. She still loved my father, but things
weren't working that well between them. I was hurt and
angry at first, but I've come to recognize that Mom can't help
what she feels. She and Betty have a close relationship, and
I spend every other week with them. It felt very strange at
first, but now it feels as normal as being at Dad and Beth's.
Some of my stupid friends at school don't understand, and
sometimes I try to hide the fact that Mom is a lesbian. I feel
like a traitor to her when I do that, but I want so much to be
normal.* Female–Mennonite Church

*Dad is gay. Mom isn't. Both of them are in relationships with
other people now. I stay at Mom's most of the time, but I can
go to Dad's whenever I want. It's awkward when Dad and
Ralph touch each other in front of other people. My friends
think it's gross, and it causes me to be embarrassed about
Dad. . . . I probably shouldn't feel that way, and I know it
hurts him when I act like I don't want him coming to my track
meets or school plays with Ralph.* Male–Episcopal Church

*I like to say that I have two moms now. Mom and Kathy have
been living with each other for three years. I spend more time
there than at Dad's. . . . A few of my friends had trouble
accepting Mom living with Kathy, but if they couldn't get over
it, I figured that they weren't really my friends anyway. If
you don't accept my parents, then you aren't going to be part
of my life. . . .* Female–Evangelical Lutheran Church

*I'm okay with the fact that my father is gay. Sometimes I
get nervous. Is it in the genes? I feel like I've got all the
heterosexual drives and desires and everything, but could
that change? I don't want to be gay because it makes life
too hard. Dad lost his job and several friends and the respect*

113

*of his parents. I couldn't stand to lose everything that he
has.* Male–Assembly of God

Most of the young people who wrote comments about having
parents who were gay saw themselves as being heterosexual.
These heterosexual young people seemed, on the whole, more
accepting of their gay parents than some heterosexual parents
were of gay sons or daughters.

Some of the most painful comments that were shared with
us came from teens with a homosexual or bisexual orientation
who had experienced significant rejection by their parents. It
appears from the comments, however, that the initial rejection
or shock sometimes diminishes with the passage of time. That
does not always happen. There are also some parents who show
strong acceptance of teens with a non-heterosexual orientation.
Consider these comments:

*My parents were shocked when I told them I was gay.
Dad asked me like three or four times in a row if I was sure.
But even in the very first conversation, they told me that I
was their son no matter what happened and that nothing
I would ever do would make them love me less. They meant
it. I know this hasn't been easy for them, but they've never
been critical of me. Dad joined PFLAG [Parents, Families,
and Friends of Lesbians and Gays] and has become an
advocate for gay rights. . . . Mom has been reading books
about the Bible and trying to get our minister to consider
the possibility that he may not understand the Bible as well
as he thinks. Both my parents have been great.* Male–
Pentecostal Church

*My parents are divorced and remarried, so I have like two
families. I first told my mom about two years ago that I
thought maybe I was bisexual. She was understanding and
very helpful to me. Then I told her husband too, and he was
like totally okay with it. I can talk with both of them about
anything, and that's helped me sort things out. . . . My
dad is another story. He and my stepmom haven't been able
to handle it. They would probably do better if I had just
told them that I was a lesbian. They could handle that better
than my being bi. But I still think bi is what I am. I spend
more and more time at my mom's house because it's safe
there. . . . I love my dad so much, and it hurts me so much
that he can't accept me as I am. It's like he thinks this is a*

reflection on him or that the divorce caused it. The divorce didn't have anything to do with it, and I don't think anybody caused it. Female–United Methodist Church

Persons Who Are Transgender

Most of us spend some time in our growing up years trying to understand what it means to be male or to be female. We live in a culture which has slightly different expectations of men and of women, and it takes time for us to decide what that means for our own lives. There are a very small number of persons who become increasingly uncomfortable in their role as a male or as a female. Those persons may actually come to believe that they were born with a biological anatomy that does not match their gender. A man may feel so much like a woman that he wishes he had been born with female genitalia; a woman may wish that she had been born with male genitalia. Such persons are referred to as transsexuals.

Some definitions may be helpful here. The PFLAG organization says that a person who is transgender is "someone whose gender identity or expression differs from conventional expectations of masculinity or femininity. Gender identity is one's internal sense of being male or female, and for most people, there is no conflict between gender identity and their biological sex."

Sexual orientation and gender identity are not the same. A person who is transgender can be heterosexual, homosexual, or bisexual. The transgender category can include:

1. Transsexuals who are uncomfortable with their gender and want to change their biological sex.
2. People who express their gender by wearing clothes of the other sex. These persons are called cross-dressers now; they were previously called transvestites.
3. People who think of themselves as a third gender and don't give weight to masculine and feminine labels.
4. "Intersexed people [formerly called hermaphrodites], who are born with ambiguous genitalia and who have a different gender identity than the one they were assigned at birth."

[The above information is based on my colleague Debra Haffner's book *Beyond the Big Talk*, Newmarket Press, 2002, pages 212-213.]

You may have heard of someone who went through a series of hormone injections and eventually a surgery in order to change from a man to a woman or from a woman to a man. Those persons seek a physical change to go with their mental and emotional identity. Many of us have difficulty understanding why someone would want to take such a seemingly radical step as to have their genitalia changed, and we may be inclined to make negative judgments about people who do so. It's difficult for us to fully comprehend the kind of pain and self-doubt that a transsexual person can experience. Consider these words from a high school senior who was part of the *Faith Matters* study:

> *Only my closest friends and my parents and brother know about this. I have never felt that I was really a male. The older I get, the more I feel like I really was supposed to be created as a woman rather than a man. That's just too strange an idea for my father to accept, but my mother and my brother are starting to understand. I keep asking my father to think what it would be like to be trapped in his male body but to think he was really female. It just makes you crazy. When I'm old enough to do it on my own and can afford it, I'm going to start the hormones and have the surgery so I can become a woman, which is who I was meant to be.*

If you have difficulty understanding what a person like that experiences, you are not alone. Those of us who do not have such issues, however, should be cautious about being judgmental toward the way that other persons feel. Should you have a friend or an acquaintance who thinks he or she is transgender, encourage that person to share openly with you what he or she is feeling. Pray for that person's well-being, and seek to be a friend to that person with whatever decisions are eventually made.

If you are such a person yourself, remember that you are not alone. There are other persons who feel the same way, and there are caring professionals who can be of help to you. Your minister, rabbi, physician, or a social worker should be able to put you in contact with such a person.

A Religious Look at Homosexuality

Few issues are as potentially divisive in faith communities as the matter of homosexual orientation and behavior. Some denominations are clearly accepting of homosexuality as orientation and behavior. Some denominations are opposed to homosexuality as an orientation, a behavior, or both. There are many others that are in continuing struggle over the issue. Official denominational positions are not always representative of what clergy and laity within the denominations believe, feel, and think.

I've attempted in this chapter to help persons with a heterosexual orientation better understand how persons with a homosexual orientation feel about themselves and about life. I've also attempted to help persons of homosexual orientation better understand that they are not alone and that there are many other youth with the same orientation for whom the faith and the church or synagogue are very important. I want to emphasize a few points and share just a few other observations before closing this chapter.

First, it is important for people who believe that homosexuality is a sin and for people who believe that it is not a sin to have respect for one another and to listen to one another. Differences of opinion on this issue run right through the middle of many congregations. If people have been brought up with the teaching that homosexual behavior is a sin, it is not easy for that position to be changed. If people are convinced that homosexuality is part of God's design and that homosexual persons are in no way sinning, then it is very difficult to accept persons with a negative view on this topic. Our congregations desperately need for people to have greater respect for one another over this issue and to do a better job listening to one another.

Second, it is my own opinion that homosexuality is a part of God's design and that homosexual persons should be fully included in the life of the congregation and in society as a whole. I know that not everyone reading this book will agree, but I want to be clear about my own position. I think that it is very rare for a person with a homosexual orientation to be able to change to a heterosexual orientation. While some persons have appeared for a short period of time to make such a change in their behavior, the change rarely lasts. It has become

117

increasingly impossible for me to not believe that homosexuality is a part of the diversity of God's created world.

No, I am not homosexual myself, and I do not, to my knowledge, have persons in my immediate family who are homosexual. I do, however, have a vast number of friends, persons I love, who do have a homosexual orientation. I respect them, I enjoy their company, and I am distressed when their rights are violated or when they are treated badly by others.

Third, remember that the years between twelve and eighteen are a time when sexual identity is being fully formed. If you are at the younger end of that age range, it is possible that you are questioning your orientation. The fact that you may, for example, have some homosexual feelings does not absolutely mean that you will end up with a homosexual orientation.

In some ways, it can be useful to think of homosexuality and heterosexuality as the opposite ends of a continuum. For example:

1	2	3	4	5	6	7

Let **1** represent a homosexual person with virtually no heterosexual thoughts or desires. Let **7** represent a heterosexual person with virtually no homosexual thoughts or desires. Then **4** would represent a person who was bisexual, who experienced both homosexual and heterosexual thoughts and desires in about equal measure. In actuality, most heterosexual people would probably be a **5** or **6**, and most homosexual persons would probably be a **2** or **3**. Few heterosexuals are exempt from having occasional homosexual thoughts, and few homosexuals don't have some heterosexual leanings.

[I developed the above scale on my own many years ago, in ignorance at the time of the Kinsey 0 to 6 scale on which 0 represents the heterosexual pole and 6 represents the homosexual pole. My scale was based on observation; Kinsey's was based on considerable research.]

There is, in my opinion, nothing wrong with a homosexual orientation. The majority of people in our culture, however, do have a heterosexual orientation. In time your own orientation will become clear.

Fourth, whether you are heterosexual or homosexual in orientation, be concerned about the justice issues for homosexuals and for other sexual minorities such as bisexuals and transgender persons. There are important issues of justice and kindness about which those of us in churches and synagogues should be greatly concerned. We should be strongly opposed to:

- Unkind and sometimes violent treatment of sexual minorities.

- Ridicule or jokes made at the expense of sexual minorities.

- Hiring practices and employment policies which discriminate against sexual minorities. This includes practices within churches and synagogues.

- Laws which discriminate against sexual minorities.

- Attitudes of hate and prejudice toward sexual minorities.

Homosexual, bisexual, and transgender persons are just as loved by God as heterosexual persons. We should as individuals and as congregations stand firmly for the rights of all people.

According to the *Faith Matters* study, even congregations that are opposed to homosexuality as an orientation and as a behavior have teenagers attending who have a homosexual orientation [unless the youth group is very small]. There are probably adults in these congregation as well who have such an orientation. These persons are not going to be open about their orientation, however, if doing so will expose them to rebukes and criticism.

Fifth, seek to learn more about the movement toward marriage equality that seeks to grant the same relationship status to two gay persons or two lesbian persons as a heterosexual husband and wife have. This is a very controversial step, and you will be hearing a great deal about it in the years ahead. More than ten denominations now allow their clergy to perform these ceremonies. A full discussion of this topic goes beyond the space available in this book. Learn all you can about the issue, think about the justice matters involved, and seek God's guidance as you begin to form your opinion on the topic.

Chapter Nine
The Bible and Religious Beliefs

I checked this concordance in the church library.
That's a big book that lists every word in the Bible
and every place it can be found. I looked up pre-
marital intercourse and oral sex and abortion and
every variation on those I could think of. But I didn't
find anything. So what is the basis for everyone
saying those things are such huge sins?

Female–Church of God

Issues about the human body and sexuality are raised beginning with the first chapters in the Bible. As shared earlier in
this book, the Genesis accounts of creation make it clear that
we are made in the image of God and that God felt everything
that had been made was "very good." The Bible does not,
however, always address our contemporary concerns in the kind
of easy-to-find-the-rule-that-applies way that we would sometimes like. The teenager quoted at the start of this chapter is
right–you won't find premarital sex, oral sex, or abortion covered
in those words in Scripture. In this chapter, I want to take a
look at the Bible as a whole as it relates to the body and sexual
issues. I also want to talk some about how churches and
synagogues have come to view and handle the topic of sexuality.

The first three chapters of Genesis give a beautiful account
of creation, including the story of Adam and Eve. If you aren't
familiar with that story, I'd encourage you to read it. Think of it
as three sections:

- Genesis 1:1–2:4 which gives the first account of
  creation.
- Genesis 2:5–2:25 which gives another account of
  creation with some more detail about the creation
  of the man and the woman.
- Genesis 3:1–24 which describes what is called the
  first sin and the awareness of the man and woman
  that they are naked.

Some people take these verses to be literally, word for word, true. Others view these accounts as conveying core truths about the nature of God and of humankind but as a more poetic description. Whichever approach one takes, it is clear that these verses are conveying to us:

- That God is the power behind all of creation.
- That what God created is good.
- That human beings have a special relationship to God and a responsibility for the world in which we have been placed.

While those verses clearly affirm the goodness of what was made, it didn't take long for things to get messed up. When they eat the fruit that had been forbidden them, Adam and Eve become aware of their own nudity; and things haven't been the same since then! Also note that the story of the first sin contains the first example of putting the blame on someone else. Adam doesn't want to take responsibility for his own actions so he blames it on Eve, "the woman you put here with me." Here are the words from Genesis 3:9-12:

The Lord God called out to the man, "Where are you?"
He answered, "I heard you in the garden; I was afraid and hid from you because I was naked."
"Who told you that you were naked?" God asked. "Did you eat the fruit that I told you not to eat?"
The man answered, "The woman you put here with me gave me the fruit, and I ate it." [TEV]

Eve in turn blames it on the serpent. God doesn't accept any of the excuses. While he forgives them and does not destroy them, he also throws them out of the garden.

The reality of sinfulness and evil in the world does not mean that God's creation is not good. The basic goodness of what God has made is beyond question. The pages of the Hebrew Bible or Old Testament and the New Testament affirm repeatedly the importance and worth of the body. The Christian faith maintains that the body is the temple of the Holy Spirit, and Christians worship a Lord who chose to become flesh, to become a human being. God obviously places great value on the body. When we try to separate our existence into physical and spiritual levels, we are forcing a distinction that is in many ways contrary to Scripture.

Whether or not we take literally the story of the expulsion from the Garden, the truth remains that we do not have the comfort or the naturalness with our bodies and our sexuality that God no doubt desired us to have. Some religious people think of the body and of sexual desires as shameful, but that view misses that God intentionally created us with our bodies and our desires. Like the story of Adam and Eve, we may sometimes make the wrong choices, but that doesn't mean that our sexuality is something bad.

Matthew 5:28 says, But now I tell you: anyone who looks at a woman and wants to possess her is guilty of committing adultery with her in his heart. [TEV] That statement means most of us are in trouble! Men and women have been looking lustfully at the bodies of others for centuries. You would be abnormal if you didn't experience such feelings. It would seem that there is an inconsistency between some biblical teachings and the manner in which God created us. Did God make a mistake?

The Scriptures of the Hebrew Bible and the New Testament stand as the basic guidelines for developing faith and making ethical decisions for most religious people. One must always be careful, however, of using particular biblical verses to argue a specific point. An earlier portion of the fifth chapter of Matthew says that we are wrong if we are angry with others or call someone else "Fool!" If those words are not softened by the biblical promise of forgiveness, we are all in trouble. We have all called others "fool" [or worse!], and we have all experienced anger.

In those verses in the fifth chapter of Matthew [a part of the Sermon on the Mount], Jesus is attempting to teach his followers that obedience to God consists of more than doing or not doing particular things. We cannot fully separate our actions from our thoughts. We should certainly not harm anyone physically, but we should also not harbor angry feelings toward them in our hearts. We should certainly not commit adultery, but we should also strive to have better thoughts within our hearts. We are not always going to succeed in those efforts, but God is always ready to forgive us and to help us.

Responsible living as a sexual person involves considering our thoughts, our feelings, our words, and our actions. And gaining a solid biblical perspective on our sexuality is only possible when we look at the Scriptures as a whole in addition to focusing on particular verses. The following guidelines may be helpful to you in doing your own biblical exploration:

First, we must recognize the historical setting of any passage in the Hebrew Bible or the New Testament. We do not follow all the requirements of the Torah [the Torah refers to the Books of the Law or the first five Old Testament books]. We do not have multiple wives and concubines. We do not stone disobedient children. There are passages in the New Testament in which Paul urges celibacy, but there are others in which Paul clearly approves of marriage and even recommends marriage. Some of Paul's teachings on celibacy relate to his personal expectation that Christ would soon return in glory [the "second coming," which still hasn't happened].

Second, we must look at biblical passages in tension with one another. The passages urging us not to be angry must be balanced with passages that suggest that one should be upset, even angry, over injustice. Christ certainly displayed anger in throwing the money changers out of the temple, and Old Testament prophets clearly showed anger over injustice and the abuse of the poor. One must also put restrictive passages on sexuality in tension with the celebration of sexuality contained in the Song of Solomon [a Hebrew Bible or Old Testament book also called the Song of Songs].

Third, we must look at biblical passages through our own powers of reason and in light of our own experiences. The Bible is the *living* word of God. The Bible was written with God's direction, but God speaks to us *now* through those words. Our reason and experience are important in making sense out of biblical passages. Stem cell research, the pill for contraception, HIV/AIDS, and artificial insemination were not known about when the Bible was written. We have to use our reason and experience to relate such topics to the things we are taught in Scripture.

Fourth, we need to recognize that some apparent omissions may have been intentional. Jesus had surprisingly little to say about sexual relationships. He did not give lengthy talks about masturbation, premarital intercourse, or homosexuality–as a matter of fact, he did not mention those topics at all. The Old Testament prophets raged against many things, but premarital intercourse and homosexuality were not among them. Yet the Old Testament prophets and Jesus had a great deal to say about how people should treat one another and about the love that should be part of all our relationships. The same rules and attitudes that apply to all human relationships should apply to sexual relationships.

A negative, repressive view of sexuality is inconsistent with the Bible. The creation passages emphasize the goodness of the body and of humankind's basic nature. The Song of Solomon is a celebration of sexuality that does not imply that the lovers are married. Many Old Testament passages on sexual expression present those activities as a normal part of life. The New Testament speaks positively and joyously about marriage. Jesus blessed the wedding at Cana.

One should also note the obvious readiness of Jesus to accept people in spite of their sexual sins or transgressions. He stopped the stoning of a woman who had been convicted of adultery. It is no accident that Jesus does not prescribe a sexual ethic, for sexual relationships are to be guided by his overall teachings.

I want to share with you some interesting biblical passages and some further information about sexuality in the Bible. These come from the Today's English [TEV] translation.

Anyone who looks at a woman and wants to possess her is guilty of committing adultery with her in his heart. [Matthew 5:28]

My lover has the scent of myrrh as he lies upon my breasts. [Song of Solomon 1:13]

About the Song of Solomon: There is nothing to suggest that the lovers are married. It is probably because they are not married that they long for a place where they can sleep together in privacy. [Song of Solomon 7:12–8:2]

The Old Testament frequently uses euphemisms such as "to know" for the sex act and "thigh" for the male genitals.

Abraham said to his oldest servant, "Put your hand between my thighs. . . [Genesis 24:2]

Look, I have two daughters who are still virgins. Let me bring them out to you, and you can do whatever you want with them. But don't do anything to these men, they are guests in my house and I must protect them. [Genesis 19:8] It would not have been good to be one of his daughters!

125

Some Old Testament passages reflect a dual ethic: a woman who commits adultery is automatically punished for violating her husband's rights. A man who commits adultery is only punished if his action infringes on the rights of another man. We do not hold to that dual standard today.

If a man is caught having intercourse with another man's wife, both of them are to be put to death. In this way you will get rid of this evil. [Deuteronomy 22:22]

In Old Testament times, concubinage was an official status. It was decidedly lower than that of a wife; and the children of a concubine did not have equal status to the wife's children– unless the concubine was taking the place of a wife who was unable to have children.

Esau had two Hittite wives [Genesis 26:34] and the granddaughter of Abraham [Genesis 28:9].

He [Gideon] had seventy sons because he had many wives. [Judges 8:30]

Jacob had two wives and two concubines. [Genesis 29:21–30:13]

Solomon had 700 wives and 300 concubines [mainly to cement relationships with other rulers].

David had several wives.

It was important in biblical times for the bride to be a virgin, and it was sometimes expected that her virginity be "proved" by the evidence of blood on sheets.

The Lord will bless you with many children, abundant crops, and with many cattle and sheep. [Deuteronomy 28:4]

Fertility in biblical times was considered a sign of God's blessing.

When a woman has her monthly period, she remains unclean for seven days. Anyone who touches her is unclean until evening. [Leviticus 15:19] This is another teaching that we do not follow today.

The Lord gave the following regulations. Do not have sexual intercourse with any of your relatives. Do not disgrace your father by having intercourse with your mother. You must not disgrace your own mother. Do not disgrace your Father by having intercourse with any of his other wives. Do not have intercourse with your sister or your stepsister, whether or not she was brought up in the same house with you. Do not have intercourse with your granddaughter; that would be a disgrace to you. [Leviticus 18:6–10]

Women are not to wear men's clothing, and men are not to wear women's clothing: the LORD your God hates people who do such things. [Deuteronomy 22:5]

Bestiality was also out! Put to death any man who has sexual relations with an animal. [Exodus 22:19]

So be happy with your wife and find joy with the girl you married–pretty and graceful as a deer. Let her charms keep you happy; let her surround you with her love. [Proverbs 5:18–20]

Don't spend all your energy on sex and all your money on women; they have destroyed Kings. [Proverbs 31:3]

A good wife who can find? She is far more precious than jewels. [Proverbs 31:10]

Marriage is to be honored by all, and husbands and wives must be faithful to each other. God will judge those who are immoral and those who commit adultery. [Hebrews 13:4]

Do not deny yourselves to each other, unless you first agree to do so for awhile in order to spend your time in prayer; but then resume normal marital relations. In this way you will be kept from giving into Satan's temptation because of your lack of control. [1 Corinthians 7:5]

1 Timothy 3:2, 12 and Titus 1:6 assume that bishops, deacons, and elders are married.

1 Timothy 4:1–4 makes it clear that marriage is good.

Paul talks some of celibacy but clearly sees that as the exception and not the norm. Now, to the unmarried and to the widows I say that it would be better for you to continue to live alone as I do. But if you cannot restrain your desires, go ahead and marry–it is better to marry than to burn with passion. [1 Corinthians 7:8–9]

As the Scripture says, "For this reason a man will leave his father and mother to unite with his wife, and the two shall become one." [Ephesians 5:31]

Some persons challenged Jesus, demanding to know what would happen when a woman who had seven husbands [each of whom died before her] went to heaven. Whose wife would she be there? Jesus responds that the nature of heaven will

be different than that: For when the dead rise to life, they
will be like the angels in heaven and will not marry. [Mark 12:25]

A crowd was ready to stone a woman who had been caught
in adultery. Jesus, however, reminded the crowd that all
people have sinned and that all stand in need of forgiveness:
As they stood there asking him questions, he straightened
up and said to them, "Whichever one of you that has
committed no sin may throw the first stone at her." [John 8:8]

Loving others and treating others as we want to be treated
becomes the highest standard for all our relationships with
other people. In the introduction to the parable of the Good
Samaritan, Jesus makes it clear that love is the way to the
life eternal. The man answered, "Love the Lord your God with
all your heart, with all your soul, with all your strength, and
with all your mind;" and "Love your neighbor as you love
yourself." [Luke 10:27]

Dear Friends, let us love one another, because love comes from God. Whoever loves is a child of God and knows God. Whoever does not love does not know God, for God is love. [1 John 4:7–8]

Meanwhile these three remain: faith, hope, and love; and the greatest of these is love. [1 Corinthians 13:13]

If you'd like to do more reading in the Bible about sexuality and
relationships, here's a listing to help you:

Genesis 1–3
Genesis 17:9–22
Leviticus 18–20
Deuteronomy 24:1–5
Judges 11:37–39
Isaiah 62:1–5
Song of Solomon
Ruth 1:1–18
Ecclesiastes 3:5
Matthew 19:1–12
Mark 3:31–34
Luke 7:36–50
John 2:1–12
John 4:16–30
John 8:1–11
1 Corinthians 3:16–17
1 Corinthians 6:12–20
1 Corinthians 13
Galatians 5:16–21
Ephesians 5:21–33
1 John 4:7–21

Nine Guidelines

Clearly people will have differing opinions when it comes to sorting out the many biblical teachings on sexuality. Do not simply "accept" or "reject" the points that follow. Study them; talk about them; and decide which ones make sense to you.

1. The body is good and sexual feelings are good. God did not make a mistake in the creation process. We have been made as God wished us to be. Our bodies have been given to us for enjoyment, and sexual feelings are a part of the goodness of life.

2. Sexual intercourse is most proper and fulfilling within the context of marriage. Adultery clearly is prohibited in both Testaments and by the teachings of the Jewish and Christian traditions. Premarital intercourse does not receive the same focus as adultery in the Bible, partly because of how early people were married and because of the absence of "dating" in the way that we know those relationships today. The obvious respect for marriage, however, leaves little doubt that the marriage covenant is where sexual intercourse was thought to belong. "Fornication" in the New Testament generally refers to any sexual activity outside of marriage, and fornication is prohibited. Now the works of the flesh are obvious: fornication, impurity, licentiousness, idolatry, sorcery, enmities, strife, jealousy, anger, quarrels, dissensions, factions, envy, drunkenness, carousing, and things like these. [Galatians 5:19–21, NRSV]

This does not mean that those who practice premarital intercourse are "doomed." It does mean that the decision to have premarital intercourse is a major one and is at best on shaky ground as far as Scripture is concerned. This is not a decision to be made lightly or without regard for some of the points that follow.

3. One should NEVER treat another person as an object. For a person who takes faith seriously, there can be no such thing as a relationship which is "just" sexual. Persons are often hurt by sexual activity which involves the depersonalization of another [and of one's self]. As you have been reading the comments of other teens in this book, you've repeatedly seen instances of people being deeply hurt when not treated with respect by another.

The expectations of males and females are not always the same. In the *Faith Matters* study, males, on the whole, did not feel as great a need to be "in love" before having intercourse as most females feel. It can become extremely tempting to tell someone else that one is "in love" with that person in order to obtain sexual cooperation. That is manipulation of the worst kind, whether done by a male or a female.

4. The body and the soul are not separate, unrelated parts. Sexual feelings should not be evaluated or acted on by themselves but should be under the control of your mind and examined in terms of your relationships with others and with God. Paul's message on union with a prostitute is revealing:

> Shun fornication! Every sin that a person commits is
> outside of the body; but the fornicator sins against the
> body itself. Or do you not know that your body is a
> temple of the Holy Spirit within you, which you have
> from God, and that you are not your own? [1 Corinthians
> 6:18–19]

Paul sees the body as a means of relating to others and believes God is concerned about those relationships. People can attempt to have relationships that are purely physical, but it generally does not work out that way. God has created us in such a way that our bodies and our souls are connected.

5. One must remember the steadfastness of God's love and forgiveness. There is no need to be ashamed of any sexual feeling. The biblical passage on not looking at another lustfully comes as a reminder that our thoughts do influence our actions and that the purest thoughts result in the purest actions. We can have many types of feelings but choose not to act on them if doing so is against our values and morals. God does not judge us severely. Note the readiness with which Jesus forgives even adultery. When we feel uncomfortable with what we have thought or with what we have done sexually, we should take those concerns to God in prayer. We may be assured that we will be comforted when we have been needlessly ashamed and that we will be forgiven when we have truly sinned.

6. The marriage relationship is of special significance, and commitment is important in all sexual relationships. Unfaithfulness to one's marriage partner involves the breaking of promises to the partner and to God. Sexual relationships are of sufficient complexity and intensity that few people can be sexually active with more than one person without paying a high psychological and spiritual price.

At the time of this writing, in most states, couples who are homosexual are not permitted to marry. Persons who are sexually active in same sex relationships, however, have the same need to be committed to one another as heterosexual couples.

7. Remember that our lives are shaped by our thoughts. You need to make intentional decisions about your values. You need to carefully assess the influences to which you expose yourself. If you spend a great deal of time with persons who take sexual relationships lightly and enjoy making sexual "conquests," it will be difficult for you to maintain a mature view of sexual relationships. You need to critically assess what you read; what sites you visit on the Internet; what you see in movie theaters and on television; and the music that you play. All these things influence our thoughts, and our thoughts in time shape our lives.

8. Remember that God does hold us accountable for what we do. We are responsible for our actions. The fact that someone else manipulated us or tempted us does not remove the responsibility from us. No supervision from others or rules from any source change this reality. Unless you are a victim of rape, there is hardly ever an excuse for producing an unwanted child or passing a sexually transmitted disease to another person. Not having oral sex or sexual intercourse is the only way to be completely safe from both pregnancy and sexually transmitted disease. If you decide to have oral sex or sexual intercourse, then you need to take appropriate precautions, which are discussed more in a coming chapter.

9. Remember that sexuality should be celebrated. Young people and adults should ENJOY their bodies and should be prepared for the enjoyment of a sexual relationship by non-manipulation, integrity, and clear value choices. Kissing, hugging, fondling, being nude with another person, oral sex, and sexual intercourse are all wonderful gifts from God. Just be sure that you are ready for a particular activity at a particular time with a particular person.

What Grade Would You Give?

Adults in general are uneasy talking about sexuality with teenagers. That uneasiness is responsible for many churches and synagogues not doing much to help young people prepare for sexual decision-making. Here are some of the reasons:

- Many adults are so uncomfortable with the topic of sexuality that they can't even talk about it with their own sexual partners. As a result, they are even more frightened of talking about it with children and teens. Adults like these need help in talking more comfortably about sexuality not only so they can do a better job helping children and teens but also so they can have better sexual relationships themselves.

- Some adults feel that if teenagers are given information about sexuality that it will make them more likely to participate in activities like oral sex and sexual intercourse. That fear is not based on reality, because good research studies continue to show that teenagers who are given accurate information are not any more likely to have sexual intercourse or oral sex than other teens. Having the information, however, does make them less likely to become pregnant or to have a sexually transmitted disease.

  In the *Faith Matters* study, we found that youth from congregations which did supply information about contraception [about 8% of the congregations] reported NO instances of pregnancy. Youth from those congregations were not any more or less likely than other youth in the study to have had sexual intercourse.

- Some adults think of sexuality as not being a spiritual concern and thus not belonging in the church or synagogue. As I've tried to show in the examination of biblical passages in this chapter, sexuality is very much a spiritual concern and should be discussed in the church and the synagogue.

Clergy, youth group advisors and teachers, and youth themselves are not in agreement on the kind of job their congregations are doing in providing sexual information and on preparing young people for marriage and parenting. The *Faith Matters* study asked all three groups to "grade" the work their congregation was currently doing as excellent, good, fair, poor, or nothing. Here are the average "grades" given by each of those groups:

	Clergy	**Advisors/Teachers**	**Youth**
Sexual information	Fair	Fair	Poor
Marriage	Fair	Good	Poor
Parenting	Good	Fair	Poor

When we talked about these differences in perspective in groups with which the initial survey results were shared, we received some comments like these:

I honestly do not know how anyone could think our church is helping you prepare for dating or marriage. I know the pastors do premarital counseling for people who've set a wedding date, but we almost never talked about these things in youth group or Sunday school.
Teen Female–American Baptist Church

Many of the kids I know, who are all black like me and go to the same school, are going to be parents before they ever get a high school degree. But the church doesn't teach us how to avoid getting pregnant, and it sure doesn't teach us what it means to be a parent. . . . We have one class at school where they ask you to carry this like robot baby around and take care of it. That's a good activity to help you see the problems of being young and pregnant. But it doesn't do anything to help prepare you to be a good parent. If nobody is going to teach us parenting skills, somebody had better teach us birth control. Teen Female–National Baptist Church

I like to think that the curriculum used in Lutheran schools gives our youth what they need. As I've been listening to some of the rest of you talk tonight, I think we might be doing a little better job than some of you because we do offer instruction through our school. But what I hear the teens here saying tonight is that we aren't creating a climate where they feel comfortable raising questions.
Pastor–Missouri Synod Lutheran Church

As the *Faith Matters* study actually looked more specifically at what congregations were doing in this area, I increasingly began to feel that the youth were more accurate in their assessment than the adults. When asked to indicate the approach to sexuality education in their congregation, here's how clergy responded:

14%   said the congregation offers a reasonably comprehensive approach to sexuality education.

49%   said the congregation offers a limited amount of information and/or discussion in existing classes or groups.

37%   said the congregation does almost nothing.

Just how comprehensive the sexuality education is even in those faith-based institutions that do offer it may be a matter for debate. While 14% of clergy felt that reasonably comprehensive sexuality education was offered, not all the youth in their congregations reported receiving all the information generally considered to be a part of comprehensive sexuality education. Fewer than 14% of all the youth responding indicated that they had received any significant information from their faith-based institutions on:

- Contraception
- Preventing AIDS
- Preventing other sexually transmitted diseases
- Rape
- Homosexuality

Youth were most likely to have received information on HIV/AIDS as a social issue, on abstinence, on dating, and on sexual decision-making. Eighty-nine percent of youth felt, however, that the information on sexual decision-making they had received was not adequate.

HIV/AIDS appeared to be a somewhat frequent discussion topic for an occasional youth class or group, but teens did not often receive information on the prevention of HIV other than under the heading of abstinence. The discussions about AIDS seem to be more as a social problem about which Christians should care than as an actual condition that could potentially happen to young people in the church. When asked "Do you know everything you need to avoid getting AIDS?", only 8.5% indicated that they did.

Rape is not a popular topic for discussion in youth classes or groups. Only 6% of the youth surveyed have participated in a church or synagogue class or group discussion focused on the topic of rape and its prevention. Most of them are also not receiving that information in school or from their parents. Almost all the females who completed the survey indicated that they needed help in knowing how to prevent rape and that they needed greater assertiveness skills. That's why this book contains a substantial chapter about the issue of unwanted sex.

Even among the 8% of the youth who have received information on contraception from their congregation, the content of that information was relatively limited. Very few youth were even aware of the existence of emergency contraception, which could be an important alternative for persons who have been raped. That's why the book you are reading offers a chapter with information on contraception.

The vast majority of youth classes and groups appear to approach the topic of homosexuality from the perspective that no one in the class or group could possibly be homosexual. That same attitude is reflected in the curriculum materials of most denominations. Thus even in those faith-based institutions where discussions about homosexuality are encouraged, the youth in the group who may self-identify as homosexual or bisexual may hear that orientation condemned without any consideration to the possibility that someone in the group has or will have that orientation. Many also have or will have family members and friends with that orientation. Some denominations like the United Church of Christ and the Unitarian Universalists take a different approach; their curriculum, *Our Whole Lives*, affirms gay and lesbian teens.

Some adult leaders in congregations are doing very good work helping teens in the area of sexuality. Consider these comments:

We had this wonderful youth group advisor when I was a freshman and a sophomore. She was a home ec teacher in one of the high schools, and she knew that we weren't getting the information we needed in any classes at school. We spent two months on Sunday evening talking about sex.

135

She gave us all kinds of information no other adult had, and she made us feel comfortable asking questions. She had the pastor come one Sunday night to talk about the Bible and sex. That was really interesting, and it was the first I discovered that the Bible actually has good things to say about sex. It helped all of us. Female Senior–Church of the Brethren

I thought I was pregnant two years ago. I didn't know who to turn to, but I remembered that our youth pastor always said we could talk to him about anything. I went to him, and he was so great. It turned out that I wasn't pregnant. THANK GOD! But the pastor helped me see myself differently than before. He helped me see the spiritual part of myself. He didn't put me down about having had sex. He just wanted me to see the big picture. And he wanted me to use birth control if I was going to keep doing it. I think that may have been the most important conversation in my life. And he like totally honored my privacy. He never told anyone, and he never made me feel uncomfortable about what I had told him. Female Junior–Church of God

You may well have been given this book by one of your parents, by your pastor or rabbi, or by a youth teacher or advisor in your congregation. Whether your church or synagogue is doing an official class on the topic or not, the fact that you have the book probably indicates there are concerned adults who are willing to deal with the topic. Of course, you may have purchased the book yourself at a bookstore. If that's the case, perhaps you should think about giving it to your parents or to your pastor or rabbi. Perhaps you can be part of helping more teens learn this important information.

Chapter Ten
Unwanted Sex

I can't exactly say that I was raped. He didn't use physical force, and I didn't shove him away. But I didn't want to do it. I kept explaining why I didn't think I was ready. No matter what I said, he just kept saying that if I loved him, I would do it with him. We would go a little further each time, and finally I let him push into me. I wish now that I'd stopped him, but I couldn't make myself do it at the time. He should have respected me more, and I should have respected myself more.

Female–Evangelical Lutheran

Some people find in sexual intercourse a connection not only to each other but also to God, who has given us the gift. Sex, under the right circumstances, can be great fun and a wonderful connection to the other person. But unwanted sex can be horrible with consequences that affect a person for the rest of his or her life.

Some of those reading these words may have already been the victims of an unwanted sexual experience as a teenager. Or you may have been a victim of sexual abuse as a child. Studies show that as many as one in three or four women and one in six to ten men have been sexually abused as children. These are extremely difficult experiences that have significant impact on the life of the victim. People who have been through these experiences need to talk with a caring adult about what has happened and can often benefit by talking to a professional counselor.

It's incredibly important that you not be responsible for another person having an unwanted experience and that you do everything possible to avoid being a victim of such an experience yourself. In this chapter, I'll share with you the experiences some other teens have had; and we'll look at ways to avoid unwanted experiences. Before continuing with the chapter, take a few minutes to reflect on this concern by writing [in the book or in your mind] YES or NO for each of the following items:

Yes or No?

_____ 1. I know someone who has been raped.

_____ 2. I have been raped myself.

_____ 3. I know someone who has had an unwanted sexual experience other than rape.

_____ 4. I have had an unwanted sexual experience other than rape.

_____ 5. I feel assertive enough to keep from doing something sexually that I don't want to do.

_____ 6. I need better communication skills for talking with a partner or potential partner about sexual decisions.

_____ 7. I need help becoming a more assertive person.

_____ 8. I know the basic things needed to avoid being in a situation in which I would be likely to have an unwanted sexual experience.

Social, Emotional, and Physical Force

Not all unwanted sexual experiences are the result of physical force. In the *Faith Matters* study, we found that social pressure and the desire to be accepted are more likely than physical force to be responsible for a teenager being pushed into a sexual experience in which he or she does not want to participate. The Evangelical Lutheran teenager quoted at the start of this chapter also had this to say:

> *I don't know what is wrong with me. Why am I so afraid to stand up for myself and to say firmly, "Stop that. Right now"? Or better yet, before anything has happened, "Don't you even think about it. We won't do that until I say it's okay, and that day may not come with you." But I start to feel like my whole world will fall apart if he rejects me, so I give him this unhealthy power over me. I wish someone could help me stop it.*

Not surprisingly, females were more likely than males to report having had unwanted sexual experiences. Females were also more likely than males to express a desire for help becoming more assertive and for help learning how to avoid rape, sexual harassment, and sexual abuse. In a discussion group about teens and sex, a female minister and mother of two teenagers shared this observation:

> *In this culture, there are still big differences between males and females in assertiveness about sex. Guys are much more inclined to ask for and push for what they want, and girls are more likely to feel that they need to nurture and please. I still don't feel like I can say "No" to my husband when he wants to do something sexually, but he says "No" to me with some frequency.*

Our culture does encourage males to be more assertive or even aggressive and females to be "nice." In sexual relationships, that can have tragic consequences. Among 11th and 12th graders, the *Faith Matters* study found that females were more than twice as likely as males to have had unwanted sexual experiences. Here's how teens responded to this question: "Have you ever had an unwanted sexual experience?"

	9th-10th Grades	11th-12th Grades
Male	6%	12%
Female	12%	31%

We asked those who reported such experiences to indicate how the pressure for the unwanted experience came:

Primarily physical pressure	12%
Primarily social or emotional pressure	76%
Uncertain	12%

Even when teens checked primarily physical pressure, they almost always indicated that social or emotional pressure was also strongly involved. The pressure can take many forms and sometimes reflects the expectations that young people feel others have. Consider this teenage girl's experience:

> *There's like this unwritten policy in my school that if you go out with somebody three times that on the fourth time you're supposed to put out. I stopped dating two different boys*

139

*because of that. Then I started going out with a boy that I
thought was very nice, and I didn't think he would be
that way. But he was. I fought him enough that he didn't
make me have regular sex, but I had to give him oral sex
to get him to let me up. . . . No one talks about this kind
of thing. No one does at school. No one does at church.
I live with Mom, and she doesn't have any idea what
goes on in my life.*

Physical force placed a role, but the "unwritten rule" in her
school was a factor in what happened to her. Such expectations
can make life difficult for males as well and females. An 11th
grade male commented:

*Beth and I have been a couple since we started high school,
and I really love her. We agreed that we weren't going to
have sex. Jesus is important to both of us, and we don't want
to do something we think is wrong. I hurt Beth really bad
because of something I didn't say. The fellows on the
basketball team are always talking about who they're
having sex with. Who gives great head. And some of them
kept pushing, wanting me to say what Beth and I were
doing. By refusing to answer a question one day, I ended
up giving the impression that Beth and I have slept together.
Then one of these a - - - - - - buddies of mine told his sister
who told Beth. Beth was so hurt. I left the team. I wasn't
going to let myself be put in that kind of situation again.*

A 12th grade male shared this perspective:

*Some of the fellows I hang with talk like sex is this
impersonal thing that you do–like the girl is just an object
instead of a person. And they talk like the goal is to do as
much as you can, whether the other person wants to do it or
not. Some of the talk is just crap. People haven't really done
everything they claim they have. But some have. And when
I'm with them, I start to feel like there's something wrong with
me because I haven't had sex yet. But the problem isn't with
me. The problem is with them.*

The teens in one of the groups in which we talked about the
survey results had a very animated discussion about the impact
of the expectations of others on what couples do when they are
together. The girls in the group talked about the tension
between getting a reputation of being "cheap" and getting the

reputation of "thinking you're better than everybody else." Those who get the reputation of being "cheap" are seen as far too ready to have sex and are not respected by others. On the other hand, those who appear not to be having intercourse or oral sex can be seen as thinking they are better than other people. Most of the teens in the group didn't want to be viewed by others as being in either of those categories. They all felt, however, that it was much better to be thought of as "better than other people" than to be thought of as "cheap."

The boys in the group agreed that there were certain girls who were viewed as being "easy." While boys might go out with girls they viewed in that way and attempt to take advantage of them, they tended not to have respect for them. They also agreed that some girls were seen as being cold and that those girls were sometimes referred to as "uptight bitches." The boys in the group acknowledged that the older you were, the greater the pressure was on you to have had sexual intercourse. Several boys felt that others would eventually start to act like there was something wrong with you if you didn't talk like you'd had intercourse or at least oral sex.

Those peer expectations create a climate in which young people can feel under pressure to have intercourse and oral sex. That pressure can cause males to be more aggressive and can cause females to be less forceful in resisting. A male parent in a discussion group where we talked about the results made this observation:

> *In some ways our society has made a lot of progress in male and female roles in the workplace. But it seems to me that we've made less in dating and sex. When I was in high school, the general expectation was that guys were looking to have sex and girls were being careful about giving it up. I'm not sure that we've moved very far beyond those stereotypes.*

And to some extent that parent is right. We haven't moved as far beyond those stereotypes as one would like–not in the face of 31% of teenage girls in the 11th and 12th grades in the *Faith Matters* study having had unwanted sexual experiences. Yet not all of the aggressiveness is on the part of males. Here are some comments from teenage males:

I was surprised to find out how much more experienced my girlfriend was. It's like she had done everything, and I'd done almost nothing. I made a fool out of myself trying to act like I knew more than I did. And we did some things that I wasn't ready for. Junior–United Methodist Church

I'm not sure how I feel about oral sex. There's something about it that makes me feel used. I don't like the taste, and I can never seem to get in a comfortable position. My girlfriend absolutely refuses to give me oral sex. She says it makes her feel degraded. But she wants it from me. I don't want her to lose interest in me, so I go along with it. It's not okay for her to be degraded, but it's okay for me to be. Sophomore–Evangelical Covenant Church

For a religious person, there are some important things that are clear:
- We are called to care more about what God thinks of us than about what others think of us.
- There are no circumstances under which it is all right for us to force someone else to do something he or she does not want. Whether the force is physical or emotional, it is not acceptable for a religious or moral person.
- It is not all right for us to let someone else push us into doing something that we are not ready to do or that we believe is wrong.
- What "everyone else" does or what our friends "expect" should not determine our sexual decisions.

Alcohol, Drugs, Love, and Rape

In responding to the first survey item on "unwanted sexual experiences," the *Faith Matters* teens defined for themselves what such an experience was. Another item asked them to be more specific in describing those experiences. The total is more than 100% for females. Many respondents had more than one type of unwanted experience:

Unwanted Activity	Males	Females
Unwanted sexual intercourse	2%	11%
Unwanted oral sex	11%	38%
Unwanted touching below the waist	15%	53%
Unwanted touching above the waist	10%	68%
Unwanted kissing	35%	62%
Other unwanted experiences	16%	19%

Of those females who had experienced unwanted sexual intercourse, almost exactly half felt that they had been raped. The others felt that they had been pushed into intercourse but did not want to describe what had happened as rape. These reasons were shared for not wanting to call the unwanted sexual intercourse rape:

- Some felt that it was not rape if they had not been physically forced to have intercourse. If the pressure was entirely social or emotional, they did not feel it had been rape.

- Some did not feel it was rape because they knew the person who was responsible for the unwanted experience. Those teens felt that "rape" is something that is done to you by a stranger. Very few teens had their unwanted experiences, of any kind, with strangers.

- Some indicated that they did not want to define themselves as "rape victims." They felt better about themselves if they accepted some responsibility for the unwanted experience.

  People have the right to decide for themselves what they want to call the experiences they have had. Unwanted sexual behaviors of any kind, however, are always wrong and should not happen. That can't be over-emphasized.

None of the males who indicated having had unwanted sexual intercourse felt they had been raped.

The number of teens who indicated that they had been personally responsible for the unwanted sexual experience of another person was less than a fourth the number who reported having such unwanted experiences. There are several possible

143

explanations for the gap between those who had been victims and those who acknowledged that they had been aggressors:

- It is possible that the teens who participated in this study were less likely than other teens to have been responsible for inflicting unwanted experiences on others.

- One teen who is sexually aggressive may well be responsible for the unwanted experiences of more than one other young person.

- Some teens may in fact fail to recognize the extent to which, through emotional or social pressure, they forced others to do something they did not want.

- Some teens may simply have been unwilling to take responsibility for their actions by admitting them even on an anonymous survey.

Comments from some teens acknowledged that it had been very difficult for them to come to see themselves as having taken advantage of another person. For example:

I screwed up. When my girlfriend and I were together, I honestly thought she was okay about everything we did. Sometimes she'd say no or push at me, but it always seemed kind of playful to me, like she was into it. When she broke up with me, she told me that I didn't respect her body and that meant I didn't respect her. At first I didn't agree. I sure never intended to pressure her. But then I started to see that I should never have gone ahead when she said no. Male–Presbyterian Church

The worst moment of my life was when my girlfriend and her mother came to our home to talk with my parents and with me. I could tell they were pissed from the moment they came in the door. My girlfriend thought I had tried to rape her. I didn't see it that way at all, but by the time she was done talking and crying I did. If they had gone to the police, my life would have been over. And I would have had it coming. I look back now and have trouble believing what I did. Male–African Methodist Episcopal Church

*Bob was two years younger than me. He was such a
hunk and had gone out with enough people that I thought
he was sexually experienced. I was wrong, and I handled
it all wrong. I made him feel inadequate and then made
him feel like he had to do what I wanted. I made too many
assumptions, and we didn't talk about things.* Female–
Synagogue

While physical force played a role, particularly in those
instances when the unwanted sexual experience was
intercourse, the social and emotional pressure and horrible lack
of communication caused the majority of the unwanted
experiences. Several factors were very clear among the teens in
our study who were a part of unwanted sexual experiences:

- Some still do not accept the concept that "No means no."
  There is a tremendous tendency, especially in the midst
  of strong sexual arousal, to ignore clear requests for
  activities to stop.

- Some, particularly females, have not learned to say "No"
  with force and conviction–ideally before sexual exploration has begun. Often "maybes" or unclear messages
  are given.

- Most teens have not talked together about what they do
  and do not want to do sexually. The sharing of affection and exploration begins, and whatever communication takes place is under very difficult circumstances.

- The desire to be accepted and loved is a major factor
  in some teens going further than they really want
  sexually. There is also a double standard at work.
  Boys are "supposed to" try to go further, and girls
  are "supposed to" stop them.

- Some of the written comments suggest that there
  are some "unwanted experiences" which only become
  unwanted later–when the sexual activity doesn't result
  in the relationship for which one of the participants
  had hoped.

  Don't let the factors which affected so many in the
  Faith Matters study affect you. Do these things:
  - Decide for yourself what you do and do not want

to do sexually in your relationships.
- When you are dating, talk with your partner about what you are and are not willing to do sexually. Listen to what your partner has to say about what he or she wants. Don't do something unless both of you feel it is all right and that you are ready for that level of intimacy in your relationship.
- Remember that NO always means NO. Never go ahead and do something when your partner says no.
- Learn how to kindly but clearly say NO to your partner. If you feel uneasy about doing this, then practice doing it in front of a mirror. Talk with your parents or a youth advisor about it. And pray about it.
- If it is clear that your partner has trouble accepting NO or has sexual expectations very different than your own, find a new partner!

Alcohol and drugs also play a significant role in unwanted sexual experiences:

> Among the teens in the *Faith Matters* study who had unwanted sexual experiences, 26.3% indicated that they were using alcohol or drugs on at least one of the occasions when they had such an experience.

Alcohol was three times more likely to be a factor than any illegal drug. In written comments and in interviews, teens talked about the significant extent to which alcohol and drugs lowered inhibitions. For example:

When I drink, I become like this totally different person. Nothing seems like a big deal, and I just want to have fun. I should never drink when I'm with a guy. Female–United Methodist

I like to drink when I'm with a girl because it helps me not be so nervous. When I'm sober, I'm this shy, uptight little boy. When I drink, I have more confidence in myself and feel like an adult. . . . The only problem is that I also lose my self-control. I've done things when I'm drunk that I'd never do sober. Male–Southern Baptist

A very candid teen in a youth group meeting made the interesting observation that she doesn't get drunk on alcohol but gets "drunk on love." She explained that she wants so much to feel that she's loved that she'll do things she would not under other circumstances. "If a boy knows enough to tell me that he loves me, then he's found the key to my heart and the key to my panties. I don't like it, but that's how I am." She said it with humor, and the group gave her an embarrassed laugh in response. The humor, however, was a mask for a very serious issue, and subsequent discussion in the group showed that she was not the only one who felt that way.

The desire for approval; the desire for love; pressure from friends; alcohol and drugs; and poor communication are all factors which can make you more vulnerable to unwanted sexual experiences.

Unwanted Sexual Experiences with Older Dates and Family

Not all the unwanted experiences of the *Faith Matters* teens were with other teenagers:

> Females who were in dating relationships
> with older males who were out of high
> school were 31% more likely to have
> had intercourse than those dating males
> in high school–and they were 21% more
> likely to have had unwanted sexual
> experiences.

Thus the study gives reinforcement to the common parental concern about high school age females dating older males. The older males are likely to be more sexually experienced and to be more assertive in what they want. [The number of high school males dating older females who were out of high school was too small for any conclusions to be drawn.] An 11th grade Presbyterian female shares these observations about the dating relationship she had as a 10th grader with a male who was a college sophomore:

> *I have a father who's eight years older than my mother, and*
> *I threw that up to them when they complained about my*
> *dating someone four years older. But now that I look back,*
> *I see that it was a mistake. Four years may not mean*

147

that much when you're thirty, but it means a lot when you're sixteen. Until he went to college, John just lived down the street from us; and I guess I had a crush on him most of my life. When he asked me to go to a movie with him when he was home on summer break, it was like a dream come true. My parents weren't going to let me go with him, but we both told them it was just a friendship thing, so they let me. Then we just kept moving ahead in small stages until he was coming home every weekend to have time with me. And I'd go visit him on campus–lying to my folks and saying I was staying with a girl there when I was with him.

He knew so much more about sex than I did. I felt uncomfortable at the time with some of the things we did, but I wanted so desperately to come across as mature that I went along with anything he wanted. Of course I see that clearly now in a way that I didn't at the time.

The biggest price was that I started living in his college world in my mind more than in high school. I started viewing my high school friends as immature and had no interest at all in the high school boys. I was pretty cruel to some people, and I'm amazed they are still. . . friends.

Her understanding of the problems of dating someone who was in college only became clear to her after the relationship ended. Most of the high school girls in the study who were currently dating males who were out of high school did not share that kind of self-awareness, even if they had gone through unwanted sexual experiences.

> If your parents are not permitting you to date a
> person who is older than you or already out of
> high school, remember that there are some good
> reasons for their concern.

> If your parents are permitting you to date someone
> who is older than you or already out of high school,
> remember that your sexual expectations and those
> of the person you are dating may be very different.
> Talk to the other person about this, and be careful
> not to be pushed into anything you don't want to
> do.

> If you are dating someone who is a more than a year
> younger than you are, you need to be especially
> careful that you do not push that person into sexual
> activity for which she [or perhaps he] is not ready.
> Obviously you don't want to do that with anyone
> you date, regardless of age; but the danger is especially
> great with someone who is more than a year younger.

Some of the worst unwanted experiences that were reported
involved adults who were much older than the teens and
generally in some kind of family relationship. This very graphic
account from an 11th grade female is particularly disturbing
because of the failure of a pastor to offer help to the teen:

*My stepfather makes me suck his d - - - after school two or
three days a week. I talked to my mother about it, and
she said I was lying. Then I told her about it right in front
of him. He denied it completely and said I was probably
making it up because he was too busy and didn't give me
much attention. . . .*

*Then I talked about it to our pastor. He talked to my
parents, and he believed my stepfather rather than me.
They don't believe that this is happening. . . . He [the
stepfather] was very angry when I talked to my mother
in front of him. Then the pastor talking to him earned
me a . . . beating. The bastard said he'd put my mother
in the hospital if I ever told anyone again. So I keep on
doing it and letting them act like they are so religious.
I'd like to bite it off, but I don't have the guts.*

The *Faith Matters* study had reports of unwanted sexual
experiences with fathers, stepfathers, stepmothers, brothers,
sisters, stepbrothers, and stepsisters. We did not have any
reports of unwanted experiences with mothers. This account
from a 12th grade male shares considerable conflict about his
relationship with a stepsister:

*My stepsister and I have been having sex with each other
every chance we get for the last two years. It's a huge
secret. Absolutely no one knows about it. We're very
careful, and we both go out with other people.*

*The first time happened because she was flirting with me,
and I responded more strongly than she expected. I ended*

up partly undressing her. She asked me not to do it, but I thought she was still kidding. . . . It was only later that I realized I'd pushed too hard. Nothing happened for about two months after that, and I spent every day scared out of my mind that she would tell her mother or my father. That would have been such a disaster. Then she really turned the tables on me. She threatened to tell them if I didn't do what she wanted me to do. The difference was that I was really, really, really willing to do anything she wanted.

So it started with her flirting. Then I forced her. Then she forced me. But there's no force going on now. We both want it. The question is what we do when we are both out of high school. If our parents hadn't married, there would be nothing wrong with our dating or even marrying each other. Maybe there still isn't, but I don't think most people could handle it. I'm not sure the two of us could handle anyone knowing about this.

The most frequently reported unwanted sexual experiences with family members involved girls and their stepfathers. Those incidents were much more frequently reported than any involving biological fathers. The inhibitions which are present in the biological relationship seem, at least among those teens who shared experiences with us, not to be as strong between stepfathers and stepdaughters. What was particularly alarming to me as I read the accounts was that several of these situations were ongoing, and the teen was not talking about it with a parent or any other adult.

Those teens who indicated that they had reported the experience and that it had stopped had most frequently talked to a parent other than the offender or in some instances to a youth pastor. They were more likely to report having visited with a youth pastor than with any other adult outside of the family.

If you are being pressured into a sexual relationship with a family member, you need to talk to someone about it and get it to stop. If you don't feel that you can discuss this with a parent, then go to a pastor or rabbi. While the youth pastor in one example shared here proved not to be truly helpful, that is the exception. Your pastor or rabbi is very likely to believe you and to take steps to help you. A teacher at school or a school psychologist or the parents of a close friend are other persons you can approach. You can also go to law enforcement authorities, though the other options given are likely to be more comfortable ones for you initially. If one adult doesn't believe you, then keep trying other adults until you find one who does.

If you have been a victim of sexual abuse and aren't sure where to turn, try calling Voices in Action at 800-7-Voice-8; www.voices-action.org.

Prevention and What to Do if Something Bad Happens

Here's an overview of some things you can do to help prevent an unwanted sexual experience. Some of these points are a review of things said earlier in the chapter.

1. Be sure you know something about the person you are dating. If someone new asks you out and you know very little about that person, be cautious about where you go on a first date. Since so many unwanted sexual experiences happen in dating relationships, knowing as much about the person you are going to date as possible just makes sense. It's probably better to get to know that person through school or church or synagogue activities or in other group situations before going out by yourself with that person. A double-date with another couple isn't a bad idea.

2. Be clear about what you do and do not want to do sexually. You should have limits on what you are willing to do sexually, at your current point in life, with *any* person. And you should have limits on what you are willing to do with a particular person at a particular time in your dating relationship. Being clear on this will help you communicate well with the other person and will help you avoid being pushed into something you do not want to do.

3. Communicate with the person you are dating about what the two of you do and do not want to do sexually before you get involved in any sexual behaviors. These are not conversations that should take place while you are in the

151

process of kissing and touching each other! You both want to be clear in advance on what you are and are not willing to do. Be considerate of the other person, and insist that the other person be considerate of you. If the other person can't accept your limits, find someone else to date.

Communication is important not only about sexual limits but about the rest of the relationship as well. If you and the other person just aren't able to communicate clearly and pleasantly with each other, then you probably need to consider a new relationship. You need to be able to talk with each other about what you are going to do when you go out, about your families, about school, about your faith, and about what is important to you in life. If you communicate well about lots of things, then communicating well about sex will not be so difficult.

4. Say NO clearly and firmly if the other person suggests or starts to do something sexually that you do not want to happen. Don't be worried about hurting the feelings of the other person. If he or she really cares about you, then that person will respect you and will want to know if there is any danger of your being pushed into something. If the person cares more about his or her own pleasure than about you, then that person is a jerk and you are better off without him or her in your life.

5. If you are under pressure from a family member or if you have been the victim of unwanted sex from a family member, you need to talk to a caring adult about it. That may be a parent, a pastor, a rabbi, a teacher, a psychologist, a social worker, or a law enforcement officer. Get help! If you are being pushed by a family member, it is not likely that you can stop it without help.

6. If someone is physically violent with you, drop that relationship immediately and tell an adult you trust what happened. Dating violence is unfortunately very common. If the person you are dating shoves you or squeezes your arm too tightly, or hits you, then that is not a safe person to be with. And it's very likely that the violence toward you will get worse over time. You need to get out of the relationship, and the other person needs counseling.

7. While most rapes involve people who are known by the victim rather than strangers, take reasonable precautions in how you live to prevent assault from a stranger. For example:

- If you feel good about your appearance, it's fun to dress in fashions that reveal your body in attractive ways. Remember, however, that some unhealthy people may think that you are sexually available because you dress in a way that they consider provocative. This is unfair, but it is sometimes a sad fact of life. Be smart!

- Watch where you park when you go to school events, the shopping mall, and other places. Try not to park too far away from where other people are.

- Don't give out your address to people you do not know. Be very careful how much information you give about yourself to persons on the Internet. Don't let someone you meet over the Internet know where you live!

- If the presence of someone makes you feel uneasy, if you start to feel like you are being followed, trust that feeling. You may be wrong, but it is better to be safe. Immediately go to where other people are.

- If someone comes too close to you and makes you feel threatened, talk in a very loud voice saying, "You are bothering me. I want you to stay away from me. Get away from me now." Use those or similar words. Your use of a loud, firm voice will make that person want to get away from you and will also bring the attention of persons who can help.

- If someone starts to use physical force on you, yell, scream, hit, bite, and kick. Don't be worried about hurting the other person–the other person deserves to be hurt. You can forgive the person when you are safe, but God wants you to do what you need to do to avoid harm. The nose and the genitals are very effective targets when it comes to physical response to a male. If you are wearing shoes with hard soles, a stomp on the foot of an attacker can also be effective.

Obviously you want to do everything possible to avoid being physically assaulted, and that's the focus of most of the advice being offered here. Some people maintain that you should not attempt to defend yourself physically from a rapist. If the rapist has a weapon, that is probably good advice. If the rapist does not have a weapon, however, a strong show of resistance from you may well make that person stop the attack and run. A good resource about this topic is Kathleen Baty's *A Girl's Gotta Do What a Girl's Gotta Do: The Ultimate Guide to Living Safe and Smart* [Rodale Press, 2003].

- NOISE is often the best weapon that a person has against an assault. Some people carry a loud whistle for protection. A whistle can do more good than a weapon, because you can use it BEFORE you are assaulted and scare the person away. Some automobiles are equipped with remote controls that can activate an alarm or the car's horn and lights. That remote control can offer you a measure of protection if you are approaching your automobile alone.

- Carrying a weapon like a knife, a gun, or a chemical spray does not necessarily make you safer. Unless you have the advantage of surprise and are very proficient with the weapon, it can be taken away from you and be used against you. Each year, many police officers, whom we assume to be skilled at self-defense, end up being shot with their own guns. Carrying a weapon is usually not a good idea; those who do carry them need to have been trained in their use.

- Some people like the confidence that they gain from taking a class in physical defense or from learning one of the martial arts.

But having shared all those things, remember that you are more likely to be assaulted by someone you know. Clear communication with people is always your best defense. If someone you know won't take a gentle no for an answer, then the other techniques can help—especially saying NO in a loud and firm voice.

If you are raped, there are some things you should be sure to do:

- Get to a safe spot before doing anything else.

- Call the police or a rape crisis center.

- Be sure not to touch your body. Washing your hands, combing your hair, applying makeup, or taking a shower can destroy evidence that might be important.

- Go to a hospital for medical care, and let your own physician know what has happened. Depending on your own values, you may want to consider the "morning-after" pill(s) [more about this in a future chapter].

- Remember that being raped is a major trauma. You will need to caring support of other people–family, friends, and professionals–to get you through this difficult experience.

- Remember that God cares deeply about you and about what happened to you. Pray about what you have been through, and seek God's help in feeling better about yourself and about other people.

Congregations Can Make a Difference

Congregations can make a difference in protecting people from unwanted sexual experiences. Training for teenagers can be provided using a resource like the book you are holding in your hands.

There are also adults in your congregation who have been victims of unwanted sexual experience. For some, it may have happened as a child; others may have had unwanted experiences as adults. Adults as well as teens can benefit from instruction about how to avoid such experiences and about how to cope with such experiences if they have happened.

The publisher of this book offers a resource by Debra Haffner called *A Time to Heal: Protecting Children and Ministering to Sex Offenders. A Time to Heal* deals with what congregations can do to keep children and all people safe from sexual abuse in the life of the church. It also gives guidance on what to do if a sexual offender wants to become involved in the life of the church. These are very real issues with which some congregations have had to deal. You may want to ask leaders in your congregation what steps are being taken to keep all people safe.

Chapter Eleven
Contraception, Pregnancy, STDs, & Abortion

*I think that I am pregnant right now. We were
committed to not having intercourse until we were
married. Then I got the chance to spend the night
at his house when his parents were gone, and it
was so wonderful to be that close for so long. We
just both started to feel like we wanted to have
sex. I thought I was still having my period and
didn't think I could get pregnant. Well, that was
wrong. I used a home pregnancy test, and it
says that I am. I'm hoping it may be wrong but
know that I have to go to a doctor and find out for
sure. What will we do? I don't want to have an
abortion, but I sure am not ready for a baby.*

Female–Missionary Alliance Church

Giving birth to a child is one of the most exciting and
wonderful things that can happen in life. An unexpected
pregnancy, however, is another matter entirely. Almost no
teenagers actually want to become pregnant–they still have high
school to finish and often want to go on to college, trade school,
the military, or some other kind of career preparation. Most
teenagers are not ready to be married or to be parents.

The female teen whose words begin this chapter faces a
dilemma that no one wants to encounter. If the home
pregnancy test is right, then she has to decide whether to have
an abortion or give birth to the child. If she decides not to have
an abortion, then she has to decide whether to keep the baby or
to have it adopted by someone else. If she decides to keep the
baby, then she has to decide how the child will be raised. Will
the father help? Does she want to marry the father? Will he
want to marry her or be involved with the life of the child? Will
her parents be able to help? Will his parents be able to help?
Will she be able to complete her education? These are very
difficult questions, and the answers will have great impact on
her life, on the baby's life, on the father's life, on her parents'
lives, and on the lives of many others.

An unexpected pregnancy or a sexually transmitted disease [STD], especially HIV/AIDS, can change your life and the lives of others in unfortunate ways. In this chapter, I want to share with you some factual information about contraception, pregnancy, STDs, and abortion. Remember that the only way to be absolutely certain of not getting pregnant and not getting a sexually transmitted disease is not to have oral sex or sexual intercourse.

In the *Faith Matters* study, we asked teens to respond to some factual questions about contraception. Before going further in this chapter, you might enjoy taking this short quiz yourself. The correct answers appear later in the chapter.

True or False?

____ 1.   The pill protects against HIV and other STDs.

____ 2.   A woman can get a shot every three months that offers protection against pregnancy.

____ 3.   Condoms fail too often to be worth using.

____ 4.   If you put a condom on incorrectly or use the wrong kind of lubricant with it, the condom will not be effective.

____ 5.   There is no emergency contraception or "morning after" pill or pills that can prevent pregnancy.

____ 6.   The pill isn't very effective in preventing pregnancy.

____ 7.   The pill often has side effects that are fairly serious.

Pregnancy and Abortion

The *Faith Matters* study found that many teens who are having sexual intercourse are not using contraception and also that many have inaccurate information about protection against pregnancy and sexually transmitted diseases. Among the teens in our study who are having sexual intercourse, 27.4% did not use any form of contraception the first time; and 19.5% did not use contraception the most recent time. Thus it is not surprising that some youth who participate in faith-based institutions have been pregnant or have gotten someone pregnant [percentages of all youth; not just sexually active youth]:

	9th-10th Grades	11th-12th Grades
Male	1.6%	3.1%
Female	1.8%	2.8%

When the percentages are looked at in terms of the youth who are having intercourse, they become more alarming with 12.9% of sexually active 9th-10th grade females and 9.9% of sexually active 11th-12th grade females reporting a pregnancy.

Half of the females responding to the survey who had become pregnant had ended it with an abortion. Several teens who had abortions commented that it was the only acceptable option given the views of their families and congregations about unwed mothers. Here's what two teenage females said about dealing with pregnancy:

I could not believe it when I got pregnant. We used a condom each time we did it except once. Apparently once was all it took! My church is pro-life and very, very down on abortion. I've helped people pass out pro-life brochures in front of a Planned Parenthood. But when I got pregnant, after I got over the shock, I didn't see many options. I shouldn't have had sex with the guy, and I sure didn't want to mess up my life by marrying him.

If I'd gone ahead and had the baby, people in my parish would have been so disappointed in me. The shame would just have killed me. And it would have been the same at school—it's a Catholic school.

I finally broke down and talked to my mother. She didn't believe in abortion either, but she agreed with me that it was the only option that made sense. And we never did tell my father that I had been pregnant or had an abortion. He couldn't have handled it. He would probably have kicked me out of the house. . . .

So now I live with this big secret. I think in my heart that God has forgiven me for what I did—for having sex so early and having the abortion. But some of my friends and the people in my parish would never forgive me if they knew. Junior–Roman Catholic Church

My guy and I had the pregnancy coming. As I look back now, I can see that we really asked for it. We didn't use any kind of birth control. Our church is so down on having sex that we were trying not to. But we'd starting making out without clothes, and then we did oral sex which didn't seem like it was quite sex. And then we'd end up doing the "real thing."

My pastor teaches that abortion is murder–one of the worst sins you can commit. My parents feel the same way. But if I had gone ahead and had the baby, there is no way that I could ever have gone to church again. I can't imagine what my parents would do if they knew. I had this older friend who acted like she was my mother so I could get the abortion. Without her I don't know what I would have done. I don't know how God feels about me now. The Bible says that we can be forgiven anything, and I know I've heard our pastor say that. But people would think I was a murderer if they knew. Maybe I am. I just couldn't make myself destroy my whole life by having the child. Sophomore–Free Methodist Church

Here are quotes from three girls who were pregnant and continued their pregnancies to term:

While I was pregnant, people at church were superficially friendly, but I could tell how much they disapproved. I finally stopped coming until I had the baby. People could deal with the baby more easily than with my being pregnant. Senior–Christian Church, Disciples of Christ

Most people in my church were pretty supportive. The older people were better than people my age. I think the older people disapproved more, but they covered it up well. People my age didn't know what to say. And I think a couple of the girls were afraid I might go after their guys because I'd be wanting a husband. Like that's so totally not where I am at. Junior–United Methodist Church

I went ahead and got married, but it's been a rough journey

*for us. We've both been able to stay in high school because
our parents help us so much, but college is going to be
impossible for both of us to do at the same time. . . . He'll
have to go to a community college, and I'll have to get a job.
We're lucky that our mothers will probably keep providing
child care. But we can't ask them to do everything for us
financially. We have to start standing on our own. . . . The
church has been very supportive to us. People have been
wonderful. We haven't felt judged or anything. I'm the one
who judges us dumb.* Senior–American Baptist Church

**Youth from congregations which did supply information
about contraception [about 8% of responding congregations]
reported no instances of pregnancy.** Youth from those congregations were not any more likely or less likely than other
youth in the study to have had sexual intercourse.   The
provision of information on contraception by the congregation
does not make teens more likely to be sexually active but does
give them protection if they are.

The fact that you are holding this book very likely means
that leaders in your congregation or your parents want you to
have the information that you need to avoid pregnancy and
STDs. **The best way to deal with the abortion dilemma is to
avoid becoming pregnant in the first place! You can do that
best by not having sexual intercourse. If you do have sexual
intercourse, then you need to use contraception.** We'll have
more information about contraception as the chapter continues.

You've heard lots of strong statements about abortion, and
many people like to speak of themselves as being "pro-life" or
"pro-choice." Being pro-choice is not the same as being pro-
abortion. Persons who are pro-choice want abortion to be
available as a legal option, but that doesn't mean they want to
see abortions happening with any frequency.

People are not in agreement about when life begins. Does
life begin at the moment the sperm joins the egg? Does life
begin when the brain and nervous system of the fetus are well
developed? Does life begin only when the fetus is capable of life
outside the mother's uterus? The Bible unquestionably affirms
the sacredness of life, but the Bible was not written to give a
scientific answer about when life begins. Religious beliefs differ
greatly on this issue.

In thinking about abortion, it can be useful to reflect on some of the real-life situations that cause people to consider that as an option. Consider these people:

- Barbara and John have a relatively low household income and have three children already. They have been using birth control, but something went wrong and Barbara became pregnant. They don't think that they can financially afford to have another child, and they don't think they can deal with giving birth to a child and then placing it for adoption. They wonder how their own children would feel about a brother or sister being placed for adoption rather than raised with them.

- Sally is an eighteen-year-old college student who was raped on a first date and became pregnant as a result. She does not want to have a child whose father is a rapist. She does not want to interrupt her education to give birth to a child. She does not want her friends to know what has happened to her. She has been in a deep depression since the rape and can't stand the idea that she is carrying the child of the person who raped her.

- Uma is fourteen years old and was raped by her stepfather. She is still in high school. She was traumatized by the ongoing sexual abuse that led up to the pregnancy, and she does not feel ready to give birth to a child.

- Marcie and Scott are married and were ready to start a family. After Marcie became pregnant, they decided to have a test called an amniocentesis that can show some abnormalities in the fetus. They decided on the test because of some history of problems in Marcie's family. The test has shown that the fetus does have an abnormality and will almost certainly be born with significant mental retardation. They do not know how to cope with this, and their insurance will not pay for the expensive care the baby would require.

- Jim and Beth are both sixteen years old and have been having sex for a few months. Beth became pregnant when a condom broke. They did not know about the availability of emergency contraception, and Beth became pregnant. Both Jim and Beth plan to go to college.

All five of those are real-life examples, with the names changed. These are cases of pregnancies that resulted from something other than people being careless about contraception. How do you feel about each situation? Dilemmas like the ones faced by these people are among the reasons that so many people are in favor of abortions being legal.

Many denominations are in support of legalized abortion: the American Baptist Churches, Christian Church (Disciples of Christ), Episcopal Church in America, Evangelical Lutheran Church in America, Jewish Reconstructionist Federation, Presbyterian Church USA, Union for Reform Judaism, Unitarian Universalist Association, United Church of Christ, and the United Methodist Church. While the Roman Catholic Church is opposed to abortion, more than half [53%] of U.S. Catholics identify themselves as pro-choice and 61% believe abortion should be legal.

It's important to think about your beliefs and values concerning abortion. Hopefully you will never be faced with the dilemma of whether or not to have one, but that decision-making will be easier if you have thought through the issues ahead of time. I personally like the statement developed by the Religious Institute on Sexual Morality, Justice, and Healing which declares that:

We seek to create a world in which abortion is safe, legal, accessible, and rare.

Many poor women around the world have abortions in very unsafe conditions. Under good clinical conditions, abortion early in a pregnancy is relatively safe. The risk of infection or damage can be substantial if done under improper conditions. Some women do not have access to a clinic for abortion, even in the United States, and some cannot afford the cost of it. When abortion is not legal or when people cannot afford the price of abortion through a clinic, then history has shown that many will turn to illegal providers of abortions or even attempt to do the abortion themselves, with horrible results.

But even though abortion should be safe, legal, and accessible, it should also be rare. Tragically it is not rare at all. Accurate statistics on abortions are difficult to obtain because of the differences with which records are kept in clinics and government agencies around the United States and around the world. The Alan Guttmacher Institute has done perhaps the best job of obtaining information about abortions. That organization estimates that the number of abortions performed in the United States has declined but still stands at over a million a year. Worldwide, there may be as many as 46 million abortions a year; and half of those are done in dangerous, often illegal situations.

The five examples given earlier of persons considering abortion [Barbara and John, Sally, Uma, Marcie and Scott, Jim and Beth] show the dilemma faced by people in difficult situations that have not resulted from being careless about birth control. The sad truth, however, is that many abortions in the United States happen each year because people have failed to be careful about the practice of contraception. Poor people in many developing countries around the world do not have access to contraception or cannot afford it.

People who are pro-choice and people who are pro-life should be able to agree that the major answer to the abortion debate is to create a society in which unwanted pregnancies almost never happen. Providing information about contraception and access to contraception in North America and around the world could make an enormous difference in the statistics on abortion. The energy spent debating the morality of abortion would be better spent promoting abstinence and contraception. The Religious Institute has another statement that I especially like:

> **The sancity of human life is best upheld when we assure that it is not created carelessly.**

What If You Think You Are Pregnant?

Many symptoms of pregnancy are unfortunately very similar to what occurs right before menstruating. Some women begin to experience pregnancy symptoms within days of conception but for others it may be a few weeks before symptoms appear. Here's a brief look at some of the symptoms:

- If a woman is usually pretty regular with periods but one doesn't arrive on time, that is the top indicator of a possible pregnancy. The missed period will likely be noticed before any of the other symptoms show. If you have been sexually active and miss a period, it's wise to take a pregnancy test.

- The increasing hormones that come with pregnancy can cause sensitive, sore breasts.

- Some light bleeding or spotting may occur about the same time a period would normally have come. This light bleeding is caused from implantation when the fertilized egg burrows into the endometrial lining.

- Extreme fatigue can be a symptom and is a result of the stress the body experiences as it adjusts to the pregnancy.

- Most women do not experience "morning sickness" until around a month after conception, but some may experience nausea and vomiting earlier.

- Some women experience increased sensitivity to certain odors. The smell of a ham sandwich or a cup of coffee or beer may trigger a gag reflex!

- Some women find themselves craving certain foods or wanting to avoid certain foods.

- Pregnancy can cause more fluid to be processed by the body which may result in more frequent urination.

The above list doesn't cover every single possibility, but a combination of those symptoms does suggest that a pregnancy test is a good idea.

Home pregnancy tests are available at pharmacies and are not very expensive, generally in the $10 to $18 range at the time this book is going to press. These tests can detect a pregnancy within a few days of a missed period, but it's very important to follow the instructions carefully. People who get a positive reading on a home pregnancy test want to go to a health care provider to get the results confirmed.

If you are pregnant, there are three options:

- You can have the baby and raise the child. If you have the baby as a teenager, you will unquestionably need a lot of help in the process if you are to complete your own education. The father can of course be a significant source of help, and your parents and other family members can also be sources of help. You have to feel ready for the responsibilities of being a parent to make this choice. The coming chapter called *A Guide to Parenting* should give you some helpful guidance on whether or not you are prepared for this responsibility.

- You can have the baby and place the child for adoption. This is an option that lets you bring the new child into the world and then turn the child over to an individual or couple who are at a point in life that they can more readily take on the responsibility of raising the child. Many people who select this option feel good for three reasons:

  - The pregnancy is not ended by an abortion. The potential new life proceeds to develop, and the mother and father have the satisfaction of knowing that the child will be raised in a loving home.

  - The adoptive parent or parents are usually persons who are unable to have a child themselves and will see the adopted child as a rich gift. The birth mother has the satisfaction of knowing that the lives of others have been enriched.

  - The birth mother does not have her life as turned upside down as would happen if she raised the child herself. After the child is born, she has the freedom to continue with her education and other plans for the future.

  There are both closed and open adoptions. In a closed adoption, the names of the adoptive parents and the birth mother are kept secret from each other. In an open adoption, the birth mother may actually select the adoptive parents. In some instances, the birth mother and the adoptive parents decide to have an ongoing relationship.

- You can choose to end the pregnancy with an abortion.
  More than 90% of abortions are performed in the first
  twelve weeks of pregnancy. One method of early abortion is called vacuum aspiration. The cervix is numbed,
  and the embryo or fetus is removed through a tube
  with vaccum suction. This is a very short procedure
  and can be done in a physician's office, a clinic, or a
  hospital.

  Another early abortion procedure is called a medical
  abortion. This is done with medicine rather than with
  instruments and can be done up to 63 days after the
  first day of a woman's last menstrual period. The
  woman is given doses of two different medicines. The
  abortion itself is generally complete within four hours
  of taking the second medication. The full process,
  however, may require one or two weeks and include
  some bleeding.

Deciding on the best option is not an easy task and is one of
the most important decisions a person will make. If you find
yourself in such a situation, you want to obtain all the guidance
and help that you can. Most teenagers want to talk with their
parents about this important decision. While a few parents may
at first be disappointed or even angry, most parents deeply love
their children and will end up doing everything they can to help
make the best decision. Generally speaking, the male
responsible for the pregnancy also needs to be part of the discussion along with his parents.

Professional guidance can be extremely important. Your
minister or rabbi or a professional counselor can often provide a
less emotional response and raise questions that those closer to
the situation may not think about. Many family planning clinics
have counselors who are trained to help people look carefully at
all the options that are present.

There are some crisis-pregnancy centers that are strongly
anti-abortion. Because of that, these centers often show films
and provide information designed to frighten a person into not
considering an abortion. Some of these centers are ethical and
will give you good information about everything except the
option of abortion. Some of these centers are so focused on
keeping people from having abortion that they will use any

strategy they can, including deceit, to keep you from considering one.

Each person's situation is unique, and it's impossible in the space available in this book to give complete information on all the options and issues that are involved. It is my opinion that the option of adoption has not received enough emphasis in recent years. Many people decide very quickly to keep and raise the baby or to have an abortion without seriously considering the possibility of adoption. If you are pregnant, I want to encourage you to consider adoption as an option. I also want to encourage you to seek advice from people who genuinely care about *you* rather than about a particular political view on abortion.

Practices and Attitudes about Contraception

We asked those teenagers who are having intercourse to share the kind of contraception they had used the most recent time. As shared earlier, 19.5% did not use any kind of contraception the most recent time. That is lower than the 27.4% who did not use contraception the first time they had intercourse, but it is still an alarmingly high figure. Condoms were the most commonly used, with 12.3% supplementing the condom with another form of contraception [most often the pill]. Over half, 57.3%, did not use a condom, which is also an alarming figure with the risk of HIV and other sexually transmitted diseases. None of the other forms of birth control listed here, except the condom, provide any protection from sexually transmitted disease. Here are the methods of contraception used for protection the most recent time by the teens in the *Faith Matters* study:

30.4%	Condom
23.3%	Birth control pills
19.5%	None
12.3%	Condom plus another method
6.5%	Depo Provera
4.3%	Other

3.7%   Withdrawal

The survey asked the teens whether or not they had all the information they needed about contraception. Among those teens who have had intercourse, only 61.9% agreed that they had all the information they need. Among teens who have not had intercourse, only 26.2% agreed that they had all the information they need. Here are some comments from teens about the use of contraception:

My boyfriend is like super ashamed to go into a store and buy condoms. I've kept saying that was his responsibility. I'm taking care of pregnancy prevention; his job is disease prevention. But he won't do it. I guess I'm going to have to get them. Female–Roman Catholic Church

Man, answering all these questions hurts me. It makes me see what a chance we're taking. We used a rubber the first time, but we haven't done anything the last three times. I didn't like the way the rubber felt, and I'm still not sure I put it on right. But that's no excuse. Male–Primitive Baptist Church

A doctor came to our youth group and talked to us about birth control. He told us how we could get it confidentially and why we should use a condom plus something else. I'm so thankful we got that information. I've been on the pill, and we always use a condom. It's the responsible thing to do. Female–United Church of Christ

My girlfriend says that she's the one who should take the major responsibility, because she would be the one who got pregnant. I suppose that's true, but I don't see that leaving me in the clear. I feel just as responsible as she does. If she got pregnant, I'd have an obligation to her and the baby. Male–Unitarian

I'm an airhead about most of my life, but not about being protected for sex. I love oral sex and intercourse, but I also know we're gambling with our futures when we do it. I take the pill, and I keep condoms in my purse. Female–United Methodist Church

I'm thankful that my girlfriend is on the pill. I would be embarrassed to buy condoms, but some of these questions make me wonder if it's a mistake not to be using a condom too. Male–Synagogue

The survey included the true/false statements related to factual information about contraception that appeared earlier in this chapter. The figures which follow are the percentages of teens who answered each question correctly. The correct factual answer is provided in parenthesis.

74%   The pill protects against HIV and other STDs. [False. It offers no protection against HIV and other STDs.]

66%   A woman can get a shot every three months that offers protection against pregnancy. [True. Depo Provera is a shot that is almost 100% effective at preventing pregnancy. The failure rate is less than 1%.]

73%   Condoms fail too often to be worth using. [False. Correctly used, condoms work 95 to 98% of the time.]

87%   If you put a condom on incorrectly or use the wrong kind of lubricant with it, the condom will not be effective. [True. Because of this, the actual user effectiveness of condoms is 86% to 90% rather than the higher effectiveness which is possible.]

26%   There is no emergency contraception or "morning after" pill or pills that can prevent pregnancy. [False. Emergency contraception within 72 hours of unprotected sex can prevent pregnancy 72 to 75% of the time.]

76%   The pill isn't very effective in preventing pregnancy. [False. The pill, taken daily, is 98 to 99% effective.]

68%   The pill often has side effects that are fairly serious. [False. The pill has been proven one of the safest drugs a person can take over the

years. It may even protect against ovarian and
uterine cancer. Some types of the pill help acne.
Most women do not gain weight on the pill.]

On every factual item, females were more likely than males
to choose the correct answer! The *Faith Matters* study also
invited teens to respond to some items concerning attitudes
about contraception and disease prevention. Here are the
percentages of females and of males who agreed with each
statement:

Talking about contraception and disease prevention before
having intercourse is a sign of respect for each other.
Females–90%   Males–81%

The girl and the guy should equally share responsibility
for contraception and disease prevention.
Females–91%   Males–78%

The girl has more influence than the guy on the kind
of contraception used.
Females–78%   Males–57%

I'd be embarrassed to go to a store and buy condoms.
Females–73%   Males–64%

Here are some more comments about contraception and
disease prevention:

*I appreciated my boyfriend asking to talk about what kind
of protection we should use. That shows he cares about
me and cares about our future.* Female–Evangelical Lutheran
Church

*My girlfriend and I had so much trouble talking about sex
and birth control. We did just fine talking about other
people having sex and about how stupid people were who
got pregnant or got HIV. But it took us a long time to talk
through our own relationship. Once we'd done it, we both
felt better. We didn't want to hurt each other, and we didn't
want to take any chances.* Male–Disciples of Christ

*If you left it up to the guy, none of them would use a rubber.
My boyfriend keeps telling me how it would feel so much
better not to have rubber between us. I tell him to think*

---

about how it would feel not to be having any sex. Female–American Baptist Church

Our youth leader had each of us sit across from a person of the opposite sex and maintain eye contact and say these words: oral sex, intercourse, clitoris, vagina, birth control pill, condom, and more. . . . At first we got red in the face and did this awkward laughing. Then it started to feel okay. It helped us feel that it was okay to talk about these things. If you're going to have sex with someone, you'd better talk about these things. Male–United Methodist Church

I had a boyfriend who told me that we didn't have to use a condom because we weren't having sex with anyone else and I was on the pill. I let him talk me out of it. Then I found out he'd been sleeping with my best friend as well as with me. With friends like the two of them, you don't need any enemies. Female–African Methodist Episcopal Church

My girlfriend and I had this deep, deep, deep talk about what it would mean to have sex with each other and about her getting on the pill and me getting condoms. By the time we talked about what we needed to do and how it would feel for her to go to the doctor for a prescription, we decided we weren't ready for sex. Male–Synagogue

This chapter has provided information about contraception in a variety of places, including the answers to the true/false quiz. I want to share some additional information with you and also a caution. Here's the caution:

Medical information about any topic is always subject to change, and I am not a medical doctor. I've done my best to research this book carefully and to have experts review the information, but I cannot guarantee it. Always rely on your physician or a good family planning clinic for the most current information about contraception.

Having given that caution, here's some more information:

Condoms work by preventing sperm from going into the vagina, mouth, or anus. Condoms are made of latex and can be very effective when properly used. The man should practice using the condom before doing so with a partner, and it's important to determine which way the condom rolls. The condom needs to be put on after the penis is erect but before it touches any part of the partner's vagina, anus, or mouth. The tip of the condom should be squeezed to force out any air. Then the condom is unrolled all the way down the penis. After the man has ejaculated and while the penis is still erect, he should withdraw, being careful that no semen is spilled. The condom should then be thrown away; never use a condom more than once.

Vaseline and heat will destroy a condom. Some people do use a lubricant that can make the condom less likely to break and more pleasant to use, and some condoms are already lubricated. You want to be sure that a lubricant is water-based [it will say so on the package]. Because condoms can break down over time, especially if kept in a warm place like a wallet, a purse, or a back pocket, it's important not to use ones that are old. Most have an expiration date on the box. Condoms are readily available at drugstores and many supermarkets. They are 86% to 98% effective at pregnancy prevention, depending on how used. If a condom should break or slip off, then you need to consider emergency contraception.

Diaphragms are flexible cups that look a little like a tiny Frisbee. They are generally folded in half and then inserted in the vagina with a jelly or cream. It opens up and covers the cervix, blocking sperm from entering the uterus. A diaphragm needs to be kept in place for about six hours after intercourse. You need to go through a physician or a family planning clinic to be fitted for a diaphragm. The effectiveness at pregnancy prevention can range from 82 to 95 percent depending on proper and continuous use.

Cervical caps are much like diaphragms but are smaller in size. They can be worn for up to 48 hours at a time and are thought by some to be less messy than a diaphragm. Like a diaphragm, these need to be obtained through a physician or a family planning clinic. The range of effectiveness at pregnancy prevention is about the same as for a diaphragm, between 82 and 95 percent depending on proper use.

Female condoms are thin, loose sleeves that are closed on one end. The closed end goes inside the vagina and covers the cervix, and the other end rests outside, creating a kind of tunnel for the penis. The female condom can block sperm, bacteria, and viruses from the vagina. This is the only birth control method besides the male condom that offers really good disease prevention. Some women choose these because they have a partner who does not want to wear a condom. These are available at pharmacies; the cost is higher than for a male condom. The effectiveness at pregnancy prevention is only about 80 percent.

The pill contains a small amount of female hormones that prevent the egg from developing in the ovary and traveling out through the fallopian tubes. The pill is taken daily for either 21 days or 28 days in a cycle. You must see a physician or a family planning clinic to get the pill, which is one of the most effective means of birth control and does not require any action at the time of intercourse. If a person does not miss doses, then the effectiveness is between 98 and 99 percent. It is important to remember, however, that the pill provides no protection against disease. If dosages are missed, the effectiveness of the pill can quickly fall. Every dose must be taken every day without fail.

Depo-Provera is a hormone injection which stops the release of eggs from the ovary and blocks sperm. The first injection is generally given during the first five days of a woman's menstrual cycle to be sure she is not pregnant. The protection lasts for three months. It must be obtained through a physician or a family planning clinic. The failure rate on pregnancy prevention is less than 1%.

The patch sticks to the skin and is placed on the stomach, buttocks, upper outer arm, or upper body once a week for three out of four weeks. It releases hormones to protect against pregnancy. At the time this book is going to print, there are no long-term published studies on the effectiveness of the patch; but it should be very high, similar to that of the pill. If it falls off, however, or if the same patch is left on for more than a week, the effectivness will decline significantly. This must be obtained through a physician or family planning clinic. *Just as this book was ready to go to the printer, I learned of a study that raises concerns about the patch delivering higher than expected doses of hormone to some persons who wear it. Information about the quality of the study and the potential problems of higher doses of hormone was not available yet. Before making a decision about the patch or any other method of contraception, always check with your physician or a reliable family planning clinic for the most current information.*

The ring is a small, flexible ring that is placed in the vagina once a month. It releases hormones to protect against pregnancy for a month at a time. It's left in place for three weeks and then taken out for a week. At the time this book is going to print, there are no long-term published studies on the effectiveness of the ring; but it should be very high, similar to that of the pill, if it is inserted properly. It must be obtained through a physician or a family planning clinic.

The sponge is made of solid polyurethane foam and contains spermicide. It is inserted into the vagina before intercourse and has a loop attached to the bottom for removal. No prescription is required for the sponge, and it is not difficult to learn how to insert it. It can be inserted hours ahead of sexual activity and can be worn for up to 30 hours. The effectiveness of it, however, is variable; and it seems to be less effective with women who have already given birth to a child. For women who have never given birth to a child, the effectiveness ranges from 84 to 90%.

Intrauterine devices [IUDs] are inserted into the uterus by a medical professional. The appear to prevent the fertilized egg from being implanted in the uterus. Some are made of copper and some of progesterone. Those made of progesterone interfere with conception. While an IUD can be very convenient and 94 to 98 percent effective, these devices also increase the risk of pelvic inflammatory disease [PID], which is a serious infection especially likely for people who have more than one sexual partner. For this and other reasons, IUDs are not recommended for women who have never had a child. IUDs seem best for women who have only one sexual partner and who have had all the children they want.

Most thoughtful couples want the best protection possible against both pregnancy and disease. As a result, many choose to combine methods, like the pill and a condom. A man also needs to wear a condom when receiving oral sex, and a woman should wear a dental dam or other barrier when receiving oral sex.

At the time this book is going to press, there have been some reports of concern about whether or not spermicides could increase the risk of HIV. Always rely on condoms rather than on spermicides. Spermicides have often been recommended for use with condoms, diaphragms, and cervical caps. The use of a spermicide can definitely help with pregnancy prevention. The sponge contains spermicide. But because of the reports of spermicides possibly raising the risk of HIV, check with a health professional before deciding to use spermicide.

Emergency Contraception is sometimes called the "morning after pill" but actually consists of two doses of four to eight hormone pills. If taken within 72 hours of unprotected sex, emergency contraception can prevent pregnancy around 75% of the time. The closer to the time of unprotected sex that the emergency contraception is taken, the better. This pill only protects against pregnancy, not against sexually transmitted disease. Some women experience upset stomachs as a result of taking this medication, but that is a lot better than getting pregnant! While some have attempted to get this available over-the-counter, a prescription is required for it to the best of my knowledge at this time. The availability of emergency contraception depends on the state in which you live. Call a family planning clinic or physician for information. **Remember that**

emergency contraception is just that–for emergency use only, not regular protection.

Natural Family Planning avoids the release of sperm into the vagina during the period of time that an egg can be fertilized. This is an approach to birth control which is recognized positively by the Roman Catholic Church. It involves maintaining a careful calendar, studying menses, recording temperatures, and observing cervical secretions. You need training from a physician or from a family planning clinic to effectively use this method. Effectiveness can cover broad range, all the way from 60% to 85%. This approach does not protect against sexually transmitted disease.

Roman Catholic young people who take their faith seriously will want to obtain information from their parish. One of the classic references for Roman Catholic youth continues to be Pope Paul VI's Encyclical Letter "On the Regulation of Birth." That Letter points out that "God has wisely disposed natural laws and rhythms. . . . which, of themselves, cause a separation in the succession of births." The Catholic Church sees husbands and wives having a mission of "responsible parent-hood," and the decision not to have a large family should be made with prayerful consideration. If contraception is to be practiced, then the Roman Catholic Church urges that it be done by recognizing the natural rhythms rather than by the use of artificial means. The Church teaches that a couple engaging in intercourse must respect the physical, psychological, and spiritual aspects of that action and of each other. The use of artificial means of birth control is seen as potentially resulting in the sexual act being taken with less seriousness and the role of parenthood being taken with less seriousness.

In the United States, vast numbers of Roman Catholics who are faithful to the Church still choose to make their own moral decisions and decide to use contraception. While Natural Family Planning does a moderately good job preventing pregnancy when carefully carried out, 85% is about the highest effectiveness that is possible. That reality combined with a desire not to have large families and to avoid sexually transmitted disease causes many Roman Catholics in this country to use other approaches to contraception than Natural Family Planning. I am not Roman Catholic, but I have many good friends who are Roman Catholics and who are Roman Catholic priests. The decision about contraception is an important one for any person and can be especially difficult for Roman Catholics. If you have a priest or a lay worker in the parish who is willing to frankly discuss these issues, that can be very helpful to a Roman Catholic young person.

HIV/AIDS and Other Sexually Transmitted Diseases

Being involved in a congregation gives no automatic protection against pregnancy, and it also gives no automatic protection against HIV and other sexually transmitted diseases. In the *Faith Matters* study, 9% of those who were sexually active reported having contracted a sexually transmitted disease.

You need to have some understanding about HIV/AIDS and the other sexually transmitted diseases that impact the lives of so many people each year. Try this factual quiz and then read the information that follows.

True or False?

_____ 1. HIV, genital warts, and herpes have something in common.

_____ 2. Teenagers are not likely to get herpes.

_____ 3. HIV is especially dangerous because it can be transmitted through water fountains, toilet seats, and other common means.

_____ 4. HIV can be transmitted by blood, vaginal fluid, semen, or breast milk.

_____ 5. Men are more likely than women to get HIV from vaginal sexual intercourse.

_____ 6. One of the advantages of anal intercourse is that you are not likely to get HIV that way.

_____ 7. A blood test is the only way to know for sure that a person has HIV.

_____ 8. Chlamydia can produce annoying sores but does
not have as serious consequences as some other
sexually transmitted diseases.

_____ 9. Men are more likely than women to show symptoms
of some sexually transmitted diseases.

_____10. Gonorrhea and syphilis were STDs that affected
older generations but are not common among
people today.

1. True. HIV, genital warts, and herpes are all viruses.
Most other known sexually transmitted diseases [STDs] are
bacterial. Antibiotics can provide good treatment for many
bacterial infections, but they are not effective against a virus.
Virus symptoms may be able to be treated, but the virus itself
cannot be eliminated from the body.

HIV stands for human immunodeficiency virus and causes
AIDS, which is the acquired immune deficiency syndrome. HIV
attacks the cells in the body that keep people healthy by fighting
infection. As a result, a person's immune system becomes
weak. People with AIDS do not die from the disease itself but
rather from other illnesses that a person without AIDS could
fight off because of having a strong immune system. HIV is a
major problem around the world.

Genital warts are also called HPV, which stands for the
human papilloma virus. This virus is closely related to the virus
that causes warts on the hands and the feet. These warts are
unattractive in appearance, but they can be more serious than
that. Some strains of HPV are associated with precancerous
cells on the cervix of the woman. Doctors generally burn off
these warts with acid or freeze them off with liquid nitrogen.
They can also be removed by laser surgery or other surgical
procedures. Those treatments do not, however, get rid of the
virus. While this virus sometimes goes into remission for long
periods of time, there is no way to know when or if it will come
back. There are 5.5 million new cases per year. HPV is very
common and is becoming more so.

Herpes or more properly herpes simplex is a virus with two
strains. Herpes simplex virus type 1 generally appears as a cold
sore on the mouth. People can develop type 1 and have it go

away without much consequence. Type 2 usually appears as painful sores in the genital area. While type 2 is the one with the bad reputation, it is also possible to get type 1 on the genitals. There is no cure, but there are antiviral drugs that may help prevent outbreaks and make it easier to live with the symptoms.

2. False. Unfortunately, teenagers actually account for between 25 and 50 percent of new infections each year. Genital herpes affects one in every four sexually active people in the United States. Genital herpes gives a very good reason for not having unprotected oral sex: a cold sore on your partner's lip can become a very serious genital infection for you.

3. False. HIV is a relatively fragile virus outside the body. It simply does not survive long enough in open air for there to be a danger of this kind of transmission. It must be in a body fluid and be transmitted from one body fluid to another. Casual contact with people who have HIV will not cause you to get HIV.

4. True. Blood, semen, vaginal fluid, and breast milk are all body fluids through which HIV can be transmitted. This means, for example, that HIV can be transmitted from a mother to a baby during birth [as blood is exchanged] and by breast feeding.

5. False. A woman's vagina has been described by some as an incubator for the virus. A woman is twenty times more likely to get HIV from vaginal intercourse than a man. Men, of course, are also at risk for HIV from vaginal intercourse.

6. False. Oral sex, anal intercourse, and vaginal intercourse are all ways of getting HIV. A latex condom is essential to preventing the transmission of HIV, and a latex barrier is needed for protection in oral sex. Anal intercourse carries a very high risk because of the possibility of tiny fissures in that part of the body.

7. True. HIV itself does not display any outward symptoms. When AIDS appears, people may show symptoms like tiredness and fever, but there is no way to know what has caused it. Blood tests are crucial to determine whether or not a person has HIV. The most common test for HIV actually measures the presence of antibodies to the virus rather than the virus itself. Antibodies develop as part of the body's effort to fight a virus. It can take perhaps three to six months from the time a person is infected with HIV until the first antibodies are produced. During that period of time, a blood test may not show the presence of HIV.

Here are a few additional facts about HIV/AIDS:

- The first cases in the United States were reported in June of 1981. Since that time, 1.5 million people have been infected with HIV in the United States and 500,000 have died of AIDS. These figures continue to increase and will no doubt be out of date by the time you are reading these words.

- Women account for a growing portion of new HIV diagnoses. The figure for women was 8% in 1985 and 27% in 2003.

- Half of new HIV infections are in persons 25 years of age and younger.

- The percentage of African Americans and of Latinos with HIV is greater than the percentage of those ethnic groups in the U.S. population. African Americans accounted for 55% of the deaths due to HIV in 2002.

- We have tremendous problems with HIV/AIDS in the United States, but the problems in Africa are even worse. Estimates vary, but it appears that AIDS has taken the lives of about twenty million people in sub-Saharan Africa since the time the epidemic began.

8. False. About half the women and a fourth of the men with chlamydia do not have any symptoms. If there are symptoms, it can include itchy genitals, rectal pain, relatively mild abdominal pain, and a burning sensation during urination. If not treated, the consequences of chlamydia can be very serious. It tends to move further into the urinary tract and the reproductive organs. A woman's uterus, fallopian tubes, and ovaries can have severe infection and damage. A man can have damage to the urethra [urine tube] and to tubes in the testicles. Infertility can be one of the results for a man or a woman. Antibiotics do a good job of treating chlamydia, when it is diagnosed early.

9. True. A woman's reproductive organs are internal, so signs of infection may not be noticed as quickly as with a man. While not all STDs have symptoms, some do including blisters, sores, warts, and other problems on the genitals; painful urination; and unusual, often foul-smelling discharges. The fact that those outer symptoms go away does not mean that the disease is gone. A man or a woman who notices symptoms needs to seek medical treatment immediately and to share the information with his or her partner.

10. False. There are about a million new cases of gonnorhea each year, and 60% of those are in persons between the ages of 15 and 24. Men may show symptoms through pain or unusual discharge in urination, but women generally do not show symptoms. This bacteria, left untreated, moves deeply into the reproductive system and can cause infertility and other serious illness. Antibiotics can cure it, though some of the newer strains of gonnorhea have been more difficult.

Syphilis has been increasing in the United States and currently affects about 150,000 people. It's transmitted through open syphilis sores or a syphilis rash. In addition to being transmitted through oral sex, anal intercourse, and vaginal intercourse, it can also be transmitted by kissing if the sores are open. Left untreated, this is a very serious disease that can result in brain damage, blindness, and death. Antibiotics work when it is caught early.

There are some other relatively common STDs in addition to those covered by the questions in the quiz:

- Crabs are actually public lice, tiny wingless bugs about the size of a pinhead. They feed on blood and like moist, hairy places like pubic hair, the anal area, and armpits. They have also been know to get into the chest, into beards, and even into eyebrows. They easily move from one person to another and can be hard to get rid of! You have to use a medicated shampoo and also have to clean and clean all your surroundings to get rid of the them.

- Hepatitis B is a virus that causes liver infection. It can be found in all the body fluids of an infected person, including saliva. It can travel through any body opening, including the mouth, but is generally spread by

vaginal or anal intercourse. It also can be passed
through shared needles. This is another virus, so it can't
technically be cured. A postexposure vaccine and the
use of immune globulin can help if treatment comes
early, but sometimes it has to run its course. Liver
cancer, cirrhosis, and death can all be results.

- Trichomoniasis, known more commonly as trich, is an
infection caused by a parasite, and there are about three
million new cases a year in the United States. This crea-
ture can live outside the body for an hour or more, so
it can be caught from using someone else's towel or
swimming suit. For the most part, however, people get
this from sexual activity. Women get an inflamed
urinary tract and cervix, and men get infections of the
urethra, bladder, testicles, and prostate gland. Your
doctor can prescribe metronidazole, which generally kills
trich. As with other STDs, both men and women have to
be treated for it.

To Prevent Sexually Transmitted Disease

- Study the information in this book and from other
sources so that you know the diseases, the symptoms,
and how they are spread.

- If you are going to be sexually active, then the man
should use a condom and the woman should use
an appropriate barrier for oral sex.

- Seek a physician's help if you have any sexually transmitted disease symptoms.

- Inform your partner immediately if you feel that you
may have a sexually transmitted disease.

- If you already have a sexually transmitted disease,
then any new sexual partner needs to be informed
about that. Don't take a chance on the welfare of
another person! There is one thing worse than the
pain of telling someone else you have a sexually
transmitted disease: that is GIVING someone else
a sexually transmitted disease.

- If you are sexually active, you need to have regular medical checkups. Remember that most STDs do not have symptoms. Tell your physician that you are having sex and ask to be checked.

And remember that the only way to be absolutely safe from pregnancy and disease is by abstaining from oral sex, sexual intercourse, and anal intercourse.

Chapter Twelve
A Guide to Dating

*There's this guy who has been maybe my closest friend
for the last four years. . . . through junior high and into
high school. He's always asking me for advice about
this girl or that girl and who he should go out with. But
it never seems to occur to him that maybe he and I should
go out together, like a couple rather than just friends. I
drop hints, but he seems clueless. I'd be more direct, but
I don't want to screw up the friendship.*

Female–Synagogue

The terminology isn't always the same: dating someone,
going out with someone, or hooking up with someone [and
"hooking up" sometimes means something a lot more intimate
than just going out on a date]. But you know what I mean. Few
experiences are more enjoyable than dating, and few
experiences can produce as much anxiety, disappointment, or
frustration!

The Bible does not, however, talk about dating as the kind of
social custom that we have in our country today. As I've shared
earlier, people generally got married much earlier in biblical
times, and marriages were often arranged or at least strongly
encouraged by parents. Young people in biblical times didn't go
out for pizza and a movie, and they didn't go to football games or
proms. On the other hand, the Bible contains lots of advice on
how we should treat other people, and that advice certainly
applies to dating relationships.

Some of those reading this chapter may have had a great
deal of experience dating. Some may have been dating for a
long time but always with the same person. Some may only
have gone out a few times. And some may not yet have gone on
a date. Some may not *want* to go on a date yet. Most reading
the chapter are heterosexual, but there are some reading the
chapter who are not. Before going further in the chapter, I want
to suggest that you take a few minutes to respond to the items
that follow to help you think about your own view of dating.

Thoughts about Dating

1. My current status on dating would best be described as
    [choose one]:
    _____ I'm not ready to date.
    _____ I'm not dating yet but would like to be.
    _____ I've dated a little but am not dating anyone right now.
    _____ I'm not dating right now because my heart has been
    broken.
    _____ I'm dating but nothing serious.
    _____ I'm in a very serious dating relationship.

2. The people I really fall for and want to date tend to be
    [check as many as apply]:
    _____ Almost the opposite of myself on most things.
    _____ Very much like myself on most things.
    _____ Older than I am.
    _____ Younger than I am.
    _____ People who aren't likely to go out with me.
    _____ Gentle and kind.
    _____ Powerful and maybe a little rough.
    _____ People my parents would love to meet.
    _____ People my parents wouldn't let in the house.

3. If you were looking for a date in the personals of the news-
    paper or Internet [not especially recommended!], which of
    these would be most likely to get your interest [check as
    many as apply]?
    _____ Searching for a lover of good times who isn't wanting
    to get serious yet.
    _____ Hot body searching for another hot body for good
    times.
    _____ Looking for someone who loves good books, good
    food, good movies, good music.
    _____ In search of someone who cares about animals,
    the environment, the poor, and God.
    _____ Some tell me I'm boring because I want to know
    about everything. If you're interested in listening
    to me, I'm interested in listening to you.
    _____ Reasonably attractive person searching for someone
    else who is attractive but agrees that isn't the most
    important thing.
    _____ Christ is the center of my life. If Christ is the center
    of your life, I'd like to get together.

4. When someone you like tells you that you look great, what is your typical response [check only one]?
    _____ "Thank you."
    _____ "Do you really think so?"
    _____ "No, I don't. I look awful today."
    _____ "Are you on drugs?"

5. When you are interested in going out with someone, how are you most likely to proceed [check only one]?
    _____ By going right to the person or calling and asking him or her to do something with me.
    _____ By starting conversations and talking with the person to get a sense of whether or not the interest is mutual.
    _____ By asking someone else to find out whether or not the person is interested in me so I know before making an approach.
    _____ By dropping hints to that person that I'd like to do something together but not coming right out and asking.

6. Suppose you've been going out with a person for a month and that person suddenly says that he or she thinks you should get married. How would you react [check one]?
    _____ If I really liked the person, I'd say YES!
    _____ I'd try to give a kind refusal, but I'd be thinking, "This person has a serious problem in thinking we know each other well enough for marriage."
    _____ I couldn't help myself; I'd have to say, "Are you out of your mind?"
    _____ I'd give a kind refusal, and I would probably stop going out with the person.

7. What are you looking for in a dating relationship at this point in your life [check as many as apply]?
    _____ I'm not feeling ready to date yet.
    _____ I'm not looking for anything serious. I just want to share some good times with someone.
    _____ I'm not looking for anyone serious, but I don't want to go out with someone I already know is a loser!
    _____ I'm not even thinking about marriage or lifetime commitment, but I want to go out with someone who understands what commitment is.
    _____ I only want to go out with someone who at least has the potential for a serious relationship.

187

The Gift of Sexuality

Getting Someone to Go Out with You

I talked with a lot of teenagers about dating in the process of doing the *Faith Matters* study. Some of them seem to get dates easily, some find it difficult, and some just plain don't try! The suggestions that follow grow out of those conversations.

First, develop good friendships with members of the opposite sex. Learn how to visit comfortably and naturally with others. You aren't going to feel confident asking someone to go out with you if you get too nervous just being around the opposite sex. [And even if you think your own orientation is likely homosexual rather than heterosexual, it's still good to become comfortable with the opposite sex.]

Church and synagogue activities and school extracurricular activities provide ideal opportunities for developing such friendships. Ask for homework help from a member of the opposite sex–but ask with no deeper intention than actually getting the help and developing a friendship. People generally see through ulterior motives.

It is perfectly possible to have close friendships with the opposite sex without ever moving into a dating relationship. On the other hand, some people end up marrying their "best friends." Learn to develop friendships for the sake of friendship. The more comfort you establish at the level of friendship, the easier it will be for you to relate to the opposite sex on a date and the easier it will be to ask someone to go out with you.

Second, remember that you will never get a date if you never ask for one. Some people are so afraid of rejection that they never ask someone to go out with them. If you don't ask or don't make it obvious that you would like to be asked, you aren't going to go out. You can plan; you can think about it; you can ask a friend whether or not a particular person might go out with you. But you finally have to work up the courage to ask.

Third, remember that male and female roles have gone through a lot of transition in our society. There is nothing wrong with a girl asking a boy for a date. A girl should not be embarrassed to do so; a boy should not feel threatened if asked by a girl. If this has not happened much in your school, you may want to go at it on a low key basis–asking a guy to share a soft drink after school, for example. But the rules are changing,

188

and girls do not have to wait patiently for the phone to ring. They can pick it up and call.

Fourth, start out on a casual basis. The best time to look for a date is not the week before the major dance of the year. Listening to a CD together, sharing supper with the family, sharing a soft drink and fries, playing miniature golf, or just working together on a school or church project may be a good way to begin.

Fifth, don't limit your choices too much. There are lots of people who want to date but aren't currently doing so. You may be frustrated because you want a date with a person who seems very popular and get nothing but rejection–yet there may be someone else just as nice you haven't thought of asking.

In many high schools, about 10% of the student body seems to be especially "popular" and sought after. But that still leaves the other 90%. People who aren't particularly outgoing or who don't take a lot of leadership roles in school activities are often overlooked. Here are some comments from teens:

Okay, I admit it. I got this fixation on this girl who was so terrific looking. I got myself convinced that I just had to have a date with her. I asked her out like three different times. She was nice, but she said no. Then I realized that I have this good friend who just lives down the street from me. For some reason, I never thought about asking her out. Then she called me and asked me if I wanted to go to a movie with her. And I thought, "Duh." We had a great time, and I realized that I like her a whole lot more than the girl I got fixated on. Male–United Methodist Church

I've always kind of taken Ben for granted. He isn't exactly running over with sex appeal, but he's really, really, really smart. The last guy I was dating treated me so badly. He kept trying to get me to have sex with him, and then I found out he was already sleeping with a friend of mine. What a fool I was. For some reason I thought about Ben and how Ben would never treat someone that way. So I called and scared Ben to death by asking him out, and it was great. Female–Synagogue

Sixth, don't be scared of blind dates as long as you know well the person setting it up. A blind date can be a disaster–but they usually aren't. One evening isn't that long a time. If the date doesn't work out all right, don't worry about it. Lots of people have met their mates on blind dates. Don't, however, go on a blind date if you don't fully trust the person setting it up; or if you do decide to do it, then do it in a public place.

If you decide to have a date with a person you've only met on the Internet, make it for a soft drink at a restaurant or some other public place. Don't take a chance with your safety. Be sure your parents know what you are doing and perhaps have a friend nearby. The Internet is terrific for many things, but it's impossible to know much for sure about someone you've only met through that medium.

Seventh, practice before asking someone out. But don't practice too long, or you'll never ask the question. Having thought through what you are going to say does help. It also helps to think about what you'll say if your request is rejected.

Eighth, take good care of your physical appearance and overall health. What is attractive to one person may not be attractive to another, but some things are universally unattractive in our culture. You don't have to use Scope, Listerine, Lavoris, or some other particular brand of mouthwash; but people with bad breath aren't going to go on many dates [at least not a second time with the same person]. Keep your hair clean; everyone looks better with clean, well-groomed hair. A good program of regular exercise can improve the health and the physical appearance of most people. If you are unhappy with yourself because you weigh more than you would like, do something about it [exercise, go on a diet, get medical guidance].

Ninth, don't make a fool of yourself by trying to impress someone else. Don't lie about athletic accomplishments or grades or your family's income or anything else. The truth will eventually come out, and your lie [or exaggeration] may make you look foolish. If a person does not like you as you are, then a long-term relationship with that person is not worth the effort!

Tenth, pray for God's guidance in connecting with a person who will be good for you in a dating relationship. We go to God for guidance with many aspects of our lives, and it's a good idea to seek that guidance in dating. Remember that in prayer it's generally better to present the need to God and seek

God's help than to tell God what should be done! You may think that a particular person would be the ideal one for you to date, but there may be someone else who would be even better.

Things to Do on a Date

Here are some of the things that teens in the *Faith Matters* study told me they enjoyed doing on dates. This list probably includes things you would never want to do on a date, but perhaps there are a couple of idea here that will be helpful:

- Do homework together.
- Listen to music together. Find out what each other likes.
- Watch television.
- Watch a DVD.
- Go out for pizza.
- Get dressed up and go to a nice restaurant.
- Go to a movie.
- Go bowling.
- Play miniature golf.
- Play regular golf.
- Go running.
- Go ice skating.
- Go roller skating at a rink or park.
- Work out in a gym.
- Go to worship services.
- Go to youth group.
- Go to a hockey game.
- Go to a basketball game.
- Go to a football game.
- Go to a baseball game.
- Go to a soccer game.
- Play sports together.
- Get ice cream.
- Go to a specialty coffee shop.
- Cook together.
- Have supper with his family.
- Have supper with her family.
- Take a walk.

- Go skiing.

- Play tennis.

- Go swimming.

- Go bike riding.

- Rake leaves for an elderly person.

- Go to a political rally.

- Take up a cause like the environment or gay rights and work on it together.

- Start a Bible study group.

- Have a picnic.

- Go to an amusement park.

- Take a drive.

- Study the Bible.

- Babysit a younger brother or sister.

- Volunteer in a soup kitchen or food pantry.

- Deliver "meals on wheels" to shut-ins.

Equal Dating

The roles of men and women in our society have changed in many ways. Marriage and dating relationships have reflected those role changes. I visited with youth in several congregational settings about ways in which dating relationships could be improved. The concept of equal dating was an attractive one to most teens. The following characteristics of equal dating are based on recommendations from teens in those congregations. They are based on what Scripture says to us about how we should treat other people. Always seek to treat the other person as you want to be treated yourself. Look through the list, and determine how you feel about the characteristics. [These can also apply to gay or lesbian couples with only minor modification.]

1. In equal dating, either person is free to ask the other out or to suggest an activity. A male doesn't have to take the responsibility all the time, and a female can take the initiative.

2. In equal dating, communication is encouraged, and impression-making is not needed. Couples discuss

192

and plan their activities together. Their goal will be to help each other have a good time rather than one trying to impress the other.

3. In equal dating, financial responsibilities are shared. Specifics with this may vary depending on who has more money, but the general goal is for both parties to participate in the cost of activities. Then no one "owes" the other anything. If there is a kiss at the end of the date, it's because both people want to do it–not because one person bought dinner.

4. In equal dating, the couple "owns" the relationship together. The couple works to be honest and to make caring decisions together. The relationship continues only if both want it to do so.

5. In equal dating, each person has a right to be an individual. He or she has a right to time alone and with other people. Each has the right to change his or her mind and to be different than he or she was in the past.

6. In equal dating, each person has the responsibility to be kind. Doors are opened by the one who reaches them first, and no one assumes that he or she has certain privileges or rights because of being male or female.

7. In equal dating, sexual decision-making is a mutual task with clear communication. Unless both persons want to do something, it doesn't happen.

8. In equal dating, both persons share their opinions on things that matter–including their values and beliefs. Both say what they really think or believe rather than what one person thinks the other wants to hear. They respect differences of opinion.

Getting Serious

Developing a serious dating relationship involves fun, intimacy, companionship, communication, and affirmation–as well as conflict, doubt, and anxiety! Sometimes the most difficult question to resolve is: "Do I want to get into a deep, long-lasting relationship with this person?" If you are facing that kind of decision, ask yourself some of these questions:

First, are your basic values and beliefs similar? In casual dating relationships, people often overlook major differences in values and beliefs. In a more serious relationship, however, these differences may become more important. Talk about your views on religion, male/female roles, sex, family life, careers, and politics. Recognize your differing viewpoints, and talk about them. If there are large gaps in the way you feel and think about things, you should decide whether or not you can live with these differences. As a relationship deepens, it often becomes more difficult to face up to conflicting values and beliefs.

Second, do you really like each other? Well, obviously you liked each other some or you wouldn't have started going out with each other. There are times, however, when a person goes out with someone else because of convenience or curiosity or even lack of a better opportunity. Sometimes there are things you just don't know about each other until you start dating. But at some point in the relationship, you need to consider the fundamental question of how well you like each other.

Third, are you able to be yourselves around each other? If you are making an effort to act a certain way and be a certain kind of person around your partner, you will probably not be happy for very long. For your relationship to grow and deepen, you both should feel relaxed and secure enough to act in a way that is natural for you and doesn't mask your true personalities.

Fourth, is a large part of your relationship centered around your sexual involvement? A relationship that is based primarily on physical contact won't stay fulfilling or satisfying for long. Although the expression of physical affection can be an important part of a close relationship, there are many other components.

Fifth, are your levels of commitment in the relationship about the same? Express your feelings about where the relationship is heading, and make sure that one person is not a whole lot more committed than the other person. Do you feel the same way about dating each other only and not going out with other people? If you see the relationship not lasting beyond high school and the other person is hearing wedding bells, that is a significant factor to be considered.

Sixth, are you sure you're ready for a change in your relationship? If you are at a point in your relationship where you feel you either have to "get serious" or "break up," you may have another option. If you don't think you want to make any strong commitments, you can continue to get to know each other and enjoy being with each other. Try to ignore the expectations of others about where you should be in the seriousness of the relationship. Play by your own rules.

Remember, if you want to deepen your relationship, you need to open yourselves up and break down some of the barriers. Share your personal beliefs, experiences, plans, and fears. Make sure the things your partner has shared with you and trusted to your confidence are never disclosed, even if the relationship ends.

Not only do you need to spend a lot of time with your partner, you also need some time apart. Develop your own interests, hobbies, and friendships. If you find it difficult to be separated for even a little while, it is likely you have grown too dependent on each other.

Dealing with Lines

Some people use lots of "lines" trying to get others to have sex with them. Most of these lines are manipulative. A person who has a healthy self-image isn't going to be trapped by tactics like these. Read the sample replies given to the "lines" below. Then come up with some of your own replies and lines.

Line: "Come on. What's wrong with having sex? Almost everybody's doing it."
Reply: "Then you shouldn't have trouble finding someone else to do it with."

Line: "I can't wait. I can't stand it. I can't delay this any longer."
Reply: "Listen!. . . . I think my mother just came in the back door."

Line: "You just lead me on. If you don't want to do it, then I'm not going out with you again."

Reply: "If the only reason you want to keep seeing me is to have sex, then I don't think you care much about me. Don't let the door hit you in the rear on the way out."

Line: "There isn't any choice, When you go out with someone for the fifth time in a row, then you have to have sex."

Reply: "I know one way out. I won't go out with you the fifth time."

Line: _____

Reply: _____

Line: _____

Reply: _____

Breaking Up

You will probably go out with several people during the course of your teenage years. You may even have two or three rather serious relationships. But, until and unless you meet *the person* with whom you want to spend the rest of your life, those relationships will change in nature. The phrase "breaking up" is commonly used to indicate the end of a dating relationship. The phrase itself probably should be changed. It implies that you and the other person will no longer have anything to do with each other. Yet, if you liked someone well enough to go out with him or her–perhaps to go out several times over a period of many months–then it is sad if the end of a dating relationship has to mean the end of a friendship. Unfortunately, we seem stuck with the phrase.

There are some signs that a relationship should end. Here are some questions to consider if you are wondering whether or not you should break up with someone:

First, how much alike are your values and goals? Are you increasingly realizing that you don't want the same things out of life? If this is the case, then you don't want the relationship to move beyond casual dating. It's time to break up if things start getting too serious, and you realize that your values and goals are vastly different. Differences may sometimes contribute to an initial attraction, but significantly differing values and goals do not result in healthy relationships over the long haul.

Second, are you simply not comfortable when you are with the other person? Sometimes one discovers fairly early in a relationship that it just isn't as pleasant as it should be. But there is security in having someone to go out with, and many of us are reluctant to give up that security. If you aren't comfortable with the other person, if you don't really enjoy being with that person, then you should not permit the relationship to continue for a long time.

Third, does the other person feel much more serious or much less serious about the relationship than you do? If so, then you need to be honest about that difference; and you probably need to think about ending the relationship. It can be extremely painful to continue a relationship for months before admitting or discovering that you just didn't have the same feelings for each other.

Fourth, does the other person want significantly more or less physical affection that you want? If so, you need to be very clear about your mutual limits. If one of you has difficulty accepting the limits of the other person, end the relationship. It's no fun to feel under pressure to "put out" or "perform" each time you're together. If you are the one who wants to get more physical than the other person wants, you need to respect that and avoid pressuring the other person. If you can't live with that, then you shouldn't continue the relationship.

Virtually none of the teens I visited with during the *Faith Matters* study felt that he or she had done a good job breaking up with someone else. Here are a few suggestions:

First, accept the fact that it won't be easy. There are no easy ways to break up with someone. Face it. It's not too hard not to ask someone out again or to decline to go out after a first or second date. But with each succeeding time together, changing the relationship becomes increasingly difficult. So the starting point is to accept the fact that it won't be easy.

Second, remember that it is even more cruel and difficult to prolong a dating relationship when you feel that you no longer want to continue. If the other person feels like you do and also wants to end the relationship, nothing will happen until one of you takes the first step. If the other person is more serious about the relationship than you are, then it is cruel to continue going out with that person and thereby fostering the notion that you are as serious as he or she is. Postponing the inevitable will only make it more painful.

Third, end the relationship by talking about it in person. Don't write a letter; don't talk on the phone; don't send a message with a friend; don't start ignoring phone calls from the other person. Sit down and talk about what you are feeling. Almost all the teens with whom I visited agreed that breaking up happens with more kindness and understanding when done in person than by any other means. If you have been developing your ability to communicate with each other all along, this will be easier than otherwise.

Fourth, try to break up in a supportive way. Affirm the worth of the other person, reinforce your friendship with the other person, and express your desire to continue being friends. Do not hold out false hope by saying "maybe sometime things will be different and we might get together again." No one can predict the future, and holding out the hope of a change back to a dating relationship usually makes it harder to accept the end of the relationship in the present. You can and should express what positive things the relationship has meant to you and your appreciation of the other person.

People often are simply not "matched" well to each other. If that weren't the case, we would all marry the first person we went out with. The fact that you are no longer comfortable going out with the other person or that you would like to be more free to go out with other people does not mean that the other person is not as good as you or is not an enjoyable person. After all, that person must have a lot of good qualities, or you would never have started going out in the first place.

Chapter Thirteen
A Guide to Marriage

I have a sister seven years older than me. She got married after her first year of college. She spent the whole year planning this beautiful wedding. About 300 people came to it, and it cost my parents as much as a new car. Then two years later the marriage was over. They spent more time planning the wedding than planning the marriage. They didn't really know each other like they thought they did.

Female–Episcopal Church

Even though divorce rates are high and some people live together for years without being married, the fact remains that marriage is a major institution in our society. Most people marry. People who get divorced generally marry someone else. And many people who have a homosexual orientation would like to have the same legal rights as heterosexual couples to marry.

While media give frequent attention to high divorce rates, the number of marriages is vastly greater than the number of divorces, and many people choose to remain married to the same person until death. Look at the Sunday newspaper and notice the number of people celebrating twenty, twenty-five, thirty-five, fifty, and even sixty year wedding anniversaries!

The Bible talks about marriage, beginning with the book of Genesis. Many are familiar with these words from Genesis 2:24: **"Therefore a man leaves his father and mother and cleaves to his wife, and they become one flesh."** The Bible does, however, say some other things related to marriage that are given less weight by most people. You have probably not heard many sermons preached on these passages:

•   The Old Testament or Hebrew Bible talks about concubines, who were women with less legal status than wives. See Genesis 25:6; Judges 8:31; 2 Samuel 5:13; 1 Kings 11:3; and 1 Chronicles 3:9 for example.

• There was also a biblical expectation that if a man dies childless, his brother must marry the widow. See Genesis 38:6-10; Deuteronomy 25:5-10; Mark 12:19; and Luke 20:28.

We do not have concubines today, and we do not expect a man to marry his brother's widow! The Bible does place importance on the marriage relationship, and most of us have heard the account of Jesus blessing the wedding at Cana of Galilee by turning water into wine for the celebration [John 2:1-11].

You may have parents or other relatives who have been divorced, and you certainly have friends whose parents have been divorced. Our society increasingly has the view that it is better for people to be divorced than to proceed with a relationship that is no longer pleasant or meaningful to them. Many biblical passages are opposed to divorce, including these: Deuteronomy 22:19; Matthew 5:32 and 19:9; Mark 10:9-12; Luke 16:18; and Romans 7:2. Most major denominations have come to accept the reality of divorce and seek to help people who are going through divorce, but "until death do us part" remains the standard for marriage in virtually all religious traditions.

There are a few biblical passages that suggest it may be better not to get married. See Matthew 19:10 and 1 Corinthians 7:7, 27-28, 32-34, and 38. In reading the Corinthian passages, remember that their author, Paul, believed that the second coming of Christ or the end of the world as people knew it was going to be happening very soon. That expectation no doubt affected some of Paul's teachings about marriage.

It is important to be clear that the Bible recognizes the validity of the single life, as those passages from Paul make clear. Not everyone feels that marriage is the right choice, and that could be the case for you. While God clearly blesses weddings and marriages, God also blesses those who choose to remain single.

Most of us, however, do get married. The Episcopal teenager quoted at the start of the chapter raises an important issue: too often people do a better job planning for the wedding than planning for the marriage. In this chapter, we want to look together at some important matters concerning marriage, and we'll end the chapter with a few comments about weddings.

I also want to point out that the issues involved in marriage and parenting are much larger than can be adequately covered in a couple of chapters of a book. My friend Holly Sprunger and I are working on a book for teenagers that focuses just on marriage and parenting from a religious perspective. You'll find information about that coming book in the final chapter of this one.

Is There "One Person" Who is Your Soul Mate?

When I visited with teenagers during the *Faith Matters* study, I discovered that many of them have been told by friends and adults that there is one "soul mate" for each person on the planet earth. Some television shows and movies focus on the search of one person for his or her true "soul mate." That means there is just one person whom God intends for you to marry, and that part of the purpose of your life is to find that one person.

This relates to a view of God's will that there is a single pathway God intends us to follow in our lives. This view says that God has already determined what career we should choose, which person we should marry, how many children we should have, and many other details of our lives. This view makes life a little like a maze with only one way out. We spend our lives trying to determine what God's plan for us is, and then we feel that we are in serious trouble if we get it wrong.

Yet many people feel convinced that they have found their one and only soul mate, get married, and then two to twenty years later feel that it was a mistake and get divorced. Did they identify the wrong soul mate? Many people train for one career in college, in the military, or in trade school and then later find that another career is a better one for them. Did they make the wrong choice the first time?

Obviously it's of great importance for us to seek God's guidance for the decisions that we make. We certainly want to be on the path that God would prefer for us, but there's another way of looking at God's involvement in our lives. God in fact is with us no matter what path we choose. Consider this view of God's will from a wonderful book by Gerald Sittser called *The Will of God as a Way of Life* [Zondervan, Grand Rapids, 2000]:

201

The will of God concerns the present more than the future. It deals with our motives as well as our actions. It focuses on the little decisions we make every day even more than the big decisions we make about the future. The only time we really have to know and do God's will is the *present moment*. We are to love God with heart, soul, mind, and strength, and we are to love our neighbors as we love ourselves. [p. 29]

If we seek to do God's will all along the way and in the small decisions as well as the large decisions, we will find that the choices we make for the future become God's will for our lives. As Sittser explains it:

God does not have one will for our lives but many wills. God does not, for example, have one person selected for you to marry whom you must "find." Instead, there are many people you could marry, if you choose to marry at all. Nor does God have one career mapped out for you that you must figure out. [p. 30]

There is a Jewish expression called *Tikkun Olam* that means "repair the world" or "fix the world." That is part of the mission to which God calls all of us. No one of us can repair the world alone; the task is far too vast. But each one of us can do our part to make the world a better place, and we can walk down many different paths and on any of those paths live faithfully to God with the result that we improve the world.

The small decisions that we make in fact pave the way for the large decisions that we make. Sittser reminds us that:

The quality of our friendships, for example, will affect our decisions about courtship and marriage. If we fail to honor and cherish friends, we will be less likely to find a good marriage partner for ourselves, to say nothing about becoming a good marriage partner for someone else. [p. 57]

God has not created a world that is one vast riddle to which we must find the right answer for our lives. Rather God has created a world with many wonderful people and many wonderful opportunities and many wonderful paths along which we can walk.

Certainly there are some choices where it is very clear that there is a particular direction God wants us to go. Should you be honest or dishonest about a particular transaction? Should you cheat on a test or accept a lower grade? Should you have sex with one person when you have already made a commitment to another person? Should you use your money only for your own pleasure, or should you share that money with those who have great needs? We usually know what we should do when faced with those decisions; what we need is the strength of character to do what we know is right.

There are many decisions, however, where there are alternative paths, each of which may be a good one for our lives. Should you ask Mary or Beth or Nina to go out with you? Should you take another math class, another writing class, or a photography class for an elective? Should you major in biology, psychology, or business? Sometimes you may feel that God gives you a nudge that helps you choose one path rather than others. Sometimes you may not feel that nudge. When you do not feel that nudge, it's generally because God is leaving the decision entirely to you.

The word love has many different meanings. I can say that I love a certain kind of food, that I love my cat, and that I love my wife. But I had better not mean the same thing each time I use that word! There is a difference between the kind of "love" that we feel when initially attracted to another person and the kind of "love" that lasts through a lifetime together. The first is based, in part, on physical attraction and the circumstances of the encounter. The second is based on deep knowledge of each other, shared values, and shared experiences. The power of sexual attraction is sufficiently great that most of us will find ourselves falling in love more than once in our lives. The first weeks of a relationship can be a time when it feels like everything is perfect. But things often change as the weeks go to months and the months go to years.

Some people feel that they "fall in love" and then later "fall out of love." We'll look more closely later in this chapter at the difference between the factors that initially attract us to someone and the factors that make for a good, lasting relationship. It's very important to remember that the fact you feel in love with someone does not necessarily mean that person is the only one who can be your soul mate.

203

And the overwhelming message of the Bible is that God is with you whatever paths you choose. Even if you make a choice that later appears to have been a wrong turn, God remains with you and helps you. If you are open to that guidance, God will help all of your paths be ones that help you repair the world and enjoy the opportunities of life.

If you get married, the person whom you choose for a spouse, if you make a true commitment to that person, will become your soul mate. It isn't a matter of finding the *one* right person. It is a matter of making a commitment to the person you choose. When you make that commitment, God helps that person become your soul mate.

Marriage and Life Goals

Take some time to think about how marriage relates to your other life goals and how you feel about marriage at this point in your life.

My present attitude toward marriage is [check one]:
   ___ that finding the right person to marry is very important for my life.
   ___ that I would probably be as happy single as married.
   ___ that I probably will get married, but I don't feel in any hurry.

Rank the following in order of their importance to you as life goals [with 1 as most important, then 2,....]:
   ___ Finding the right person to marry.
   ___ Choosing the right career.
   ___ Taking good care of my physical appearance and heath.
   ___ Having a good time.
   ___ Sharing God's love with others.
   ___ Making the world a better place.
   ___ Being a good friend to other people.
   ___ Having children and being a good parent.
   ___ Trying to do God's will in my life.
   ___ [your choice:]_____

In the first column that follows, rank the characteristics listed in order of their importance in *attracting* you to a person whom you might ask out [with 1 as most important, then 2,.....]. In the second column, rank the same characteristics in order of their importance to you in a person whom you might *marry* [with 1 being most important, then 2, ...]. As you do this, think about the difference between those things that attract us to another person and those that make for a lasting relationship.

_____ _____	Intelligence.
_____ _____	Physical appearance.
_____ _____	Values similar to mine.
_____ _____	The ability to make me feel good about myself.
_____ _____	Commitment to God.
_____ _____	Ability to earn a good income.
_____ _____	Willingness to stand up for others.
_____ _____	Good communication skills.
_____ _____	Loves children.
_____ _____	Honest.
_____ _____	Other _____

Marriage isn't for everyone, but the likelihood remains that most who read this book will eventually get married. What kind of person will you marry? The exercise you just completed asked you to rank some characteristics in terms of their importance in *attracting* you to someone and in terms of importance as traits in a person you might *marry*. There obviously are some differences between what attracts us to another person and the traits that we would like to find in a potential marriage partner.

Being aware of the differences between the factors that cause initial attraction and the factors that make for a lasting relationship is an important part of making good decisions. The fact that you feel a strong attraction to a particular person does not necessarily mean that is a person with whom you should develop a long term relationship. As shared earlier in this book, sexual activities can be very powerful and can generate very strong emotions. Some people find themselves in sexual relationships with people they don't especially enjoy when fully clothed! When that happens, it's generally because they don't have the kind of shared values and deeper commitment that make for a lasting relationship. It's very hard, however, to stop a relationship once people have begun sharing intense sexual activity. It's almost always healthier to let the relationship develop gradually and not to begin sharing intense sexual activities until both people feel the relationship is moving to a deeper level in other ways as well.

When Is A Person "Ready" for Marriage?

No person can tell another when he or she is ready for marriage. You have to answer that question for yourself. I do want to suggest some guidelines that can help you determine whether or not you are ready for marriage personally–and whether or not a particular person is the right one for you.

1. Do you feel secure in your personal values and goals? Do you know what you want out of life? Are you clear about where marriage fits in with your other priorities in life? For most people, this point is not reached before sometime in their twenties. One of the major reasons that so many teenage marriages have trouble is that most people experience significant change in values through the course of life; and those changes are often dramatic in the early young adult years. You can marry someone at eighteen years of age whose values are quite similar to your own and then discover at the age of twenty-five that you have grown apart.

2. Are you able to be financially independent of your family and of your prospective mate's family? Though there are exceptions, it is still safe to say that most marriages have a bad start if heavy financial support must come from one set of parents or the other. If college is an important goal for you and if your parents are paying for your college expenses, you want to delay marriage until you finish college.

3. Do you love the other person enough to put that person's happiness and welfare above your own? People who take their faith seriously recognize that we are called in all relationships to do unto others as we would have them do unto us, or to love others as we would have them love us. There are circumstances and relationships in which a person of faith places the good of another person above his or her own pleasure or gain. That kind of love is central to a healthy marriage. If you do not feel that way toward your prospective partner, then you are either not ready for marriage yet *or* your partner is not the right one for you. If your partner doesn't feel that way toward you, then you for sure need a different partner. Don't marry someone who isn't capable of putting your needs ahead of his or her own needs, and don't marry someone for whom you aren't willing to do the same.

4. Have you spent a lot of time with the other person? Do you know what characteristics of the other person irritate you or drive you crazy? If you can't identify any such characteristics, then you probably don't know the other person well enough. If you can identify dozens of such traits, you may need to reconsider. Talk about your differences. What adjustments are you willing to make? How good is your communication? Can you genuinely say what you feel and want to the other person?

5. Does the other person make you feel good about yourself, and can you help that person feel good about himself or herself? If you're going to spend the rest of your lives together, you need to be good for each other.

6. Are you in basic agreement on matters of faith? Do you share the same values about what marriage means and about what family life should be like? Look at the marriage ritual of your denomination. Do you both agree on the questions asked in that ceremony? Can you honestly commit your lives to God as well as to each other in the marriage relationship? Are your basic values about life in agreement with each other?

7. Do you both agree that marriage is for "keeps"? We live in a time in which there are many divorces. Many religious institutions recognize that there are circumstances in which it is better for persons to have a divorce than to continue making each other miserable. But that is not the desired outcome of marriage. If you start your marriage uncertain about how permanent your relationship will be, then you have two strikes against you from the beginning. You need a high mutual commitment to a marriage that will last and be enjoyed for the rest of your lives.

Divorce brings a high price for the couple and for any children that they have. Many of those reading this book have parents who have been divorced. You may well be living now in a single parent household or with stepparents. All these are situations that can be very nurturing and loving. The young people who responded to the *Faith Matters* survey whose parents had been divorced were all doing okay with their lives, but 73% of them wished their parents were still together.

8. Do you understand the extent to which your own parents have influenced your expectations of marriage, and does your prospective partner understand the same thing about his or her own parents? For most of us, our parents are primary role models for how we will relate in marriage and as parents. We aren't "trapped" or "doomed" to repeat the mistakes of our parents, but we cannot escape being strongly influenced by them. Dealing realistically with this concern can save you grief and trouble later.

9. Do you genuinely love each other? NOT are you sexually attracted to each other? NOT can you get along with each other? NOT do your families think your marriage will be a good one? NOT are your friends getting married? But do you genuinely love each other and feel confident your love will grow over time? Unless the answer to this question is yes, the other questions really don't matter.

In the United States, the average age for women at the time of their first marriage is 25; for men, it's 26. In Canada, the figure is 27 for women and 29 for men. There has been a definite trend toward people getting married at an older age than with some past generations. In general this trend seems beneficial because it means people know themselves better and are more secure in their own values before entering into a marriage relationship.

Perhaps in part because people are delaying getting married, there are also large numbers of couples who are cohabiting before marriage or instead of marriage. According to the National Center for Health Statistics, unmarried cohabitations are not as stable as marriages. The probability of a first marriage ending with separation or divorce within five years is 20%. The probability of a premarital cohabitation breaking up within five years is 49%. After ten years, there is a 33% probability of a first marriage ending but a 62% probability of a cohabitation ending.

Many of those reading this book will at some point in time consider cohabiting with someone they are not yet ready to marry. This trend among young adults tends to make parents absolutely crazy! And almost all denominations disapprove of cohabiting with a person to whom one is not married.

I'll risk the disapproval of many adults reading this book by saying that I think it is better for people to cohabit than for them to enter into a marriage for which they are not ready. But it's important to recognize, as already shared, that unmarried cohabitations definitely are not as stable as marriages. If you aren't ready to make the commitment to marriage, you need to think about and pray about whether or not cohabiting is a step that will truly help your relationship with another person. It may be beneficial to wait longer before cohabiting or marriage.

The Physical and Spiritual Dimensions

In an important survey of Roman Catholic young adults several years ago, Fee, Greeley, and other researchers found that "prayer and sexuality are intimately connected. Expressions of human love relate strongly and positively to expressions of love for God" [*Young Catholics in the United States and Canada*, p. 51]. That study found that couples who reported their sexual relationship as excellent also reported that they pray together on a daily basis. There was a clear relationship between the strength of the religious life and the strength of the sexual relationship.

Does that mean religious people make better lovers and better mates? Perhaps so. The Christian faith teaches that God did indeed become flesh. The Jewish and Christian faiths portray the body as good. **The Gospel of John speaks of the Word, which is Christ, becoming flesh and dwelling among us [John 1:14], and the Scriptures also speak of husband and wife becoming one flesh together [Genesis 2:24 and Matthew 19:5].**

The Jewish and Christian faiths do not have the kind of diminished view of the human body that has been part of some other religions. As already shared in this book, Paul refers to the body as the temple of the Holy Spirit [1 Corinthians 6:19]. That's a strong statement about the importance of the body! And the Bible acknowledges that the relationship between a man and a woman should be a source of pleasure. The Song of Solomon speaks, without apology, of the physical pleasure that a man and a woman find in each other.

God does bless the marriage relationship, and there are both physical and spiritual dimensions within that relationship. If our bodies are temples of the Holy Spirit, then there is no such thing as a "just physical" relationship. We must also be concerned about the Spirit within us and the Spirit within the other person. The most fulfilling sexual relationships are ones that grow out of deep commitment. Meaningful sexuality is the outgrowth of a meaningful relationship–not the cause of a meaningful relationship.

As some earlier chapters of this book have shown, a sexual relationship with a person who is insensitive and uncaring is not a pleasant experience. Good communication skills, commitment to each other, and deep concern for each other maximize the pleasure of intimate sexual contact, especially sexual intercourse. Marriage provides the environment in which a couple can continue to grow in their love for each other, in their ability to communicate with each other, and in their ability to physically express the love which they feel.

When two people recognize that God is present in their relationship, they open themselves to all the good things that God wants to do for them. That includes the gift of physical pleasure.

That doesn't mean that religious spouses get on their knees beside the bed and pray before getting into bed to have intercourse. Sexual arousal doesn't generally work that way, and not many of us can concentrate on prayer when sexually aroused! It does mean that religious partners take seriously the spiritual dimension of their relationship and recognize the value of taking time to pray together, to worship together, and to share regular devotions together. As they grow closer to each other in that dimension, they will find their physical pleasure with each other increasing as well. Their communication skills go up, they deepen in genuine concern for each other, and they open their lives more fully to the presence of God.

God has blessed us by permitting us to become partners in creation. Sexual intercourse is the means by which we share in the creative process, even though prudent couples generally use contraception because they don't want to risk pregnancy each time they enjoy sex together! God is very much present in the sexual relationship between two people, and there is no way to separate the physical and spiritual dimensions. That's why the most meaningful sexual relationships occur in marriage. And that's why those who deepen the spiritual life find physical pleasure increasing as well.

Some people reading this chapter are gay. Marriage has been viewed in most of our religious traditions and by society as a whole as being a heterosexual institution. Yet, as shared briefly in Chapter Eight of this book, there is a growing movement toward "marriage equality," which seeks to grant the same relationship status to two gay persons or two lesbian persons as a hetero-sexual husband and wife have. Options for gay people may change in the years ahead. Heterosexual people are often uncomfortable with the idea of marriage equal-ity but need to give the issue prayerful consideration.

And a Few Thoughts about Weddings

You've probably attended at least a couple of weddings. It's even possible that you've been part of the wedding service of a good friend or a family member. Weddings can be wonderful celebrations, filled with excitement and times of significance. The opening quote in this chapter from the young woman who is in the Episcopal Church, however, is accurate in saying that it is possible to spend more time planning the wedding than planning the marriage. Here are a few thoughts about weddings:

First, remember that the decision to get married should be a mutual decision. Movies and television dramas take great pleasure in coming up with creative ways for the man to ask the woman if she will marry him. Engagement rings are pulled out of pockets, hidden in pieces of cake or glasses of champagne, or slid down strings.

Men have asked women to marry them in front of family members, in front of crowds at concerts, and even in front of people at sporting events. Talk about pressure! How can someone say "No way" to a marriage proposal made in front of a large number of people?

If you feel it is important to you to have the man be the one to ask the question and the woman be the one to respond, be sure that this only happens after you've had many conver-sations about what it would be like to be married. The question should not be coming as a complete surprise, and the answer should already be known. Otherwise it represents too much pressure on the woman to make a positive response. A couple should have talked about their mutual religious beliefs, what marriage means to them, what they feel family life should be like, and many other topics already covered in this chapter before they approach a decision to get married.

And if the man is going to select the engagement ring that the woman is going to wear, they should have done some looking together ahead of time so that he knows what kinds of rings she likes. Once the ring has been chosen and presented, there is no gracious way for her to say she would have liked something different to wear for the rest of her life. No woman wants to say, "Honey, some people may think that's a beautiful ring, but it's not staying on my finger for the next fifty years. We've got to get something different."

When the man purchases the ring without consultation and makes a proposal without prior conversations and shared planning, he's taking tremendous power in the relationship. And then the woman has the burden of whether or not to accept. It's much healthier for the couple to share more fully in the entire process of deciding to get married. Increasing numbers of couples go shopping together for the engagement ring and the wedding bands.

Engagement rings and wedding bands can also be extremely expensive. The cost of the rings, however, is not an indication of the love that two people feel for each other. Don't let the pressure of what your friends have done or of what the jewelry salesperson says make you spend more money than you can afford. That leads to another important observation about weddings. . . .

Second, weddings have become a BIG, BIG business with a lot of people making a lot of money from them. Your minister, rabbi, or other person conducting the service doesn't make a lot of money; and most churches and synagogues have very reasonable fees or no fees at all. But wedding planners, florists, photographers, stores selling bridal gowns, tuxedo rental companies, reception facilities, musicians, caterers, printers of invitations, restaurants, limousine companies, travel agencies [which make honeymoon arrangements], and others make a great deal of money from weddings. Weddings can be extremely expensive costing as much as or more than a very nice, new automobile.

There are magazines exclusively devoted to the topic of weddings, and each spring you can count on several television programs focused on various aspects of wedding planning. Weddings are also popular topics for television dramas and for motion pictures. All these sources of information create the impression that a person simply must have a large, elaborate wedding.

The truth, however, is that some of the nicest weddings are very simple and not especially expensive. For example:

• A couple who live in Chicago decided they wanted only their closest friends and family members at their wedding. They decided to have their service in a beautiful outdoor location on Lake Michigan. The location they wanted was part of a university campus, and there were no fees for a small service being held there. Twenty-two friends and family members came to the service, which was conducted by a minister who was a member of the family. The bride and groom wore clothes that they liked but did not purchase anything new to wear for the service. Guests were asked to dress casually. After the wedding, everyone went to a favorite restaurant for dinner and then to a condominium for wedding cake. The meal was the only significant cost of the service. The condominium was the back-up location for the service had it been raining–but they had a lovely day! A family member took the photographs, which turned out great!

• A couple who did not like crowds decided that they only wanted half-a-dozen people to be at their wedding. They asked the minister to come to the home in which they would be living and do a private service for them. Then everyone who was present went out for dinner. It was a very simple, very nice service. The bride purchased a new dress that she could wear on other occasions as well; the groom wore a suit he already had. One of the guests took the photographs.

• A couple wanted a nice wedding in a church but did not want to spend a fortune on the reception. They had a rather traditional wedding with three attendants each and a flower girl. The church organist provided the processional and recessional music. After the wedding, the reception was held in the church's Fellowship Hall, for which the only fee they paid was for custodial clean-up. They did not have a meal served but instead had a beautiful wedding cake, nuts, candy, punch, and coffee. The church's tape system was used to provide the music during the reception.

The couple had been to many weddings themselves at which meals were served that seemed, to them, very mediocre in quality, even though they knew a great deal of money had been paid for the food. They also observed that several people got drunk at the receptions, and they did not want that to happen at their wedding.

They were a little concerned that some of their 150 guests would think that they were being "cheap" by not having a meal served and by not having a band for the reception. That turned out, however, not to be the case. People liked the simplicity of the reception and also liked not having to drive to another location after the service. The cake and the punch were delicious, and people had a great time visiting. Several of their friends indicated that they would have simpler weddings themselves after seeing how nice this one was.

Third, remember that the service itself needs at least as much thought as the photography arrangements, the bridal gown selection, the reception planning, and the honeymoon arrangements. There is a tendency for people to put more thought into the other parts of the wedding celebration than into the planning for the service itself. While there are secular weddings done by justices of the peace and other public officials, the fact that you are reading this book makes it likely that you will want a religious service, conducted by a clergyperson. You want to give careful thought to the music you want included, the Scriptures you would like read, and the vows you are going to take. Many couples find it meaningful to write their own vows.

Some people like the tradition of having the bride "given away" by the father. There are others who prefer that both parents have a role in that presentation. And there are others who feel that this tradition feels too much like the daughter is the property of the parents. You want to think about the extent to which you want parents to participate in the service itself.

The service is a time in which you and your partner make commitments to each other and also to God. It can also be a time when the family and friends who are present share in prayers for blessings on your marriage. It can be an important time to celebrate God's love for all of us as well as the love for one another which results in the decision to marry.

Fourth, try to think "out of the box" on all phases of wedding planning. We understandably are influenced by weddings that we have attended or in which we have participated. That's normal. Be careful, however, that you don't get caught in the trap of feeling that you must do your wedding the same way as other people have done their weddings. And be especially careful not to feel that you need to do something more elegant or more elaborate than others have done, as though weddings were a competitive sport.

One couple had been planning a fairly traditional, rather large wedding to be held in an area church with a reception to follow in the ballroom of a hotel. They started calculating the cost of everything that they wanted and realized that it would be over $25,000. Then they asked themselves an interesting question: "How many of the people who will come to the wedding will still be connected with us five years after the wedding?" They decided it was not likely that many would be and began to question having such a large service.

They decided instead to have a simpler service at a favorite vacation location and to only invite thirty people, who were family members or very close friends. They knew that people would have some expense going to the vacation location, but they planned the wedding at a time when people could combine attending the service with some vacation time of their own. They scheduled the service far in advance so that people would have time to make arrangements. They arranged to have the service in a church and to have a wedding dinner in an historic restaurant nearby. While the expenses per person were higher, the actual cost of the wedding was far lower than the more traditional service would have been because of the restricted invitation list.

215

A couple who had become engaged to each other while serving as counselors at a summer church camp decided to have their wedding service at the same location during the comparable week of the summer a year later. Their service was attended by all the campers that week, most of whom had been present the summer they got engaged; and they also had friends and family come for the day. The service was held outdoors, with the camp chapel as backup had it rained. The camp staff worked with them to have a picnic following the service. Everyone dressed very casually with most of the campers in t-shirts and shorts. The bride wore a simple gown and was barefoot. The groom wore slacks and a silk shirt. It was a very memorable service for everyone and not very expensive.

A small church had a couple who were engaged and had very little money. As the couple visited informally with people in the congregation, there was a growing movement to help them have a wonderful wedding without much money being spent. A member of the congregation volunteered to coordinate the wedding. The service was held in the church. A member made the wedding gown for the bride, and another member bought a new suit for the groom. The reception was held at the church and was a potluck, with everyone who attended bringing a dish to share. Two members of the congregation made the wedding punch and the wedding cake. An elderly member of the congregation remembered that she still had the wedding rings of her parents, who had been deceased for years. She gave those rings to the couple. It was truly a wonderful service, made all the more meaningful by the help that so many people gave.

When planning a wedding and all the accompanying activities, couples need to think about what will make the service and the rest of the experience most meaningful to them. Give special thought to ways in which you may be able to have a memorable wedding with greater simplicity rather than making the experience so costly. You may also come up with some creative ideas like the wedding in the vacation location or at the summer camp.

And remember to spend more time planning the marriage than planning the wedding!

Chapter Fourteen
A Guide to Parenting

Being a parent is the most important job I'll ever have.
But I wasn't ready for this job. I wasn't ready to have
sex, I wasn't ready to be pregnant, and I sure wasn't
ready to raise a child. I know I got pregnant and had
a child too early, but my friends who are four and five
years older don't know any more than I do about how
to raise a child. There ought to be a required course.
I would never have made it without my parents.
Female–African Methodist Episcopal Church

The young woman just quoted was seventeen years old at the time I interviewed her as part of the *Faith Matters* study. She had a son who was eleven months old. When she learned that she was pregnant at sixteen, she determined that she did not want to marry the father. As she put it, "I did one dumb thing in having sex too early and not using birth control. I did another dumb thing in having sex with someone I didn't even like at the time. I wasn't going to make it worse by doing another dumb thing and marrying the loser."

She was initially frightened about how her parents would react and feared they might kick her out of the house. While they were disappointed that she had sexual intercourse at such a young age and that she hadn't used contraception, they loved her deeply and helped her at every stage. All three of them agreed that abortion felt morally wrong, and they didn't want to see the baby adopted. She went ahead and gave birth to the child, and her parents were helping her in raising him. She dropped out of school for one semester when she gave birth, and then she returned to school with her mother and her grandmother helping with childcare.

She felt poorly prepared to take care of the child and was deeply thankful for the help of her parents. She's right about several things:

- Her life would have been better if she had not had sexual intercourse so early. It would also have been better if she had used contraception. And she cer-

tainly should not have had intercourse with someone
she didn't even like at the time!

- Being a parent is the most important job that many of
us will ever have. That doesn't mean our vocations are
unimportant, but raising a child is an enormous responsibility. It can also be a great pleasure when we are
prepared for the experience.

- Our society tends not to give us much training for the
tasks involved in being a parent. How does a baby
develop? When can a baby eat solid food? What does
it mean when a baby cries? When does a baby need
to go to the doctor? How should a child be taught
to use the toilet? When should you start teaching a
child about God? Most of us need instruction to know
the answers to questions like those. And those are
just a few of the many that arise in parenting a child
from birth through college or trade school graduation.

As shared in the last chapter, my friend Holly Sprunger and
I are writing a book called *Marriage and Parenting: A Guide
for Religious Teens*. We don't mean by the title that teens are
ready to get married or to be parents! But teens are certainly
ready to learn more about marriage and parenting. The earlier
we learn these things, the more likely we are to make good
decisions about getting married and having children.

Waiting to Have a Child

There are some very important reasons why parenting is
best done later in life and in a marriage relationship. This
doesn't mean that teens are "bad parents," and it certainly
doesn't mean that single parents can't be good parents. Gay
and lesbian couples can also be good parents. But consider
with me some of the reasons for waiting until older to have a
child and for having that child with a loving life partner:

- A family can expect to spend $235,670 on a child born
in 2003 until the time that child turns eighteen years
of age. That's the latest figure available from the USDA
Center for Nutrition Policy at the time this book is going
to the printer. It costs a lot of money to raise a child!
Delaying parenthood until your education is complete

and your career is underway is the responsible way
to go, and it's also easier. You don't want to be worried
about money all the time, and you certainly don't want
to deprive your son or daughter of something needed.

- Kids, especially babies, are a lot of work; they are
  dependent on adults for everything. When first born,
  a baby wants to eat every two or three hours, and someone has to be awake to feed the child and change the
  resulting diapers! As they grow, someone must bathe
  them, shop for and wash their clothes, buy and prepare
  their food, take them to doctor's appointments, and see
  that they attend school and do homework. Sharing the
  work is much easier than doing it all alone.

- Having kids can dramatically change your life. Unless
  you are someone who spends virtually every evening at
  home, get ready to feel tied down. Eating in restaurants,
  going shopping, going to movies, working out, and all
  the other things people enjoy doing outside their homes
  can be more difficult if not impossible, depending on the
  age of the child(ren). Babysitters are not always available or affordable. There is much fun to be had when
  you are a teenager and a young adult; you should enjoy
  that phase of life before having children. That doesn't
  mean children aren't fun, but it's a very different experience.

- Having a child can be very stressful even for the most
  patient parent who is in a deeply committed relationship. It's much easier for you and better for the child
  to have a partner in parenting who will be with you
  through hard times as well as good times.

- Infants born to teens are two to six times more likely
  to have a low birth weight than those born to mothers
  age 20 or older. Low birth weight is associated with
  infant and childhood disorders and a higher rate of
  infant mortality. Low birth weight babies are more
  likely to have organs that are not fully developed,
  which can result in complications. [You can learn
  more about this at the website www.womenshealth
  channel.com/teenpregnancy.]

- Having a child is also wonderful. Holding a newborn
child for the first time, seeing the first smile, hearing
the first laugh, and watching the first steps are unfor-
gettable experiences. Seeing a child grow and thrive
as a result of one's love and hard work can be immense-
ly gratifying and rewarding. Sharing in that experience
with another person adds an extra element of enjoyment.

- Teens who have a child while still in high school find
it much more difficult to graduate and are less likely
to go on to college or trade school. With education
so necessary for a good-paying, relatively secure job,
being a teen parent can severely limit a person's
future.

- Children deserve to be wanted and loved from the very
start. While people who have unplanned pregnancies
can still be good parents, it's far better when the child
is planned and wanted *before* the pregnancy happens!

An eighteen-year-old male from an American Baptist
congregation shared what it was like to be the father of a baby:

*When my girlfriend got pregnant, I at first just wanted
her to have an abortion so we wouldn't have to deal
with what this would do to our lives. But that felt like
it was a selfish thing to do, so we had got married and
had the baby. I don't know if we did the right thing.
I mean, like, we should have had the baby rather than
an abortion. But maybe we should have let someone
adopt her. I love her and love her, but our lives are so
out-of-control. I'm stressed all the time, and sometimes
I'm not as nice to my wife or to our baby as I know I
should be. I've never hit our baby, but I've shaken her
too hard, and I'm like so thankful that she wasn't
damaged by it.*

*We never have enough money, even with help from
my parents. I didn't finish my senior year of high
school. I dropped out to work full-time and took night
classes so I could pass the test for a degree. My wife
still hasn't gone back to school. She takes care of the
baby during the day and then works when I'm able
to take care of the baby. We work and feed the baby*

*and clean up poop and work and feed the baby and
clean up poop. That's what life has become like for
us–filled with poop.*

Twelve Characteristics of Good Parents

All right. I've made my best case for why you should wait
until you are older and married before having a child. Now let's
consider what it means to be a good parent. Most of those
reading this book will in time decide to have children, and that's
a wonderful experience. It isn't too early to start thinking about
some of the characteristics of good parents. My friend Holly
Sprunger helped me identify these characteristics:

1. Good parents are patient and understanding. The
colicky baby [who seems to cry all the time for no apparent
reason], the toddler who takes forever to get dressed, and the
moody teenager can all be frustrating. But they just are the way
they are at that particular stage, and they need to be treated
with patience and understanding rather than anger.

Being a patient person results from several things:

*   We can be more patient when we understand how
    children develop and what they need at a particular
    stage. Babies cry a lot because that is the only major
    way they have to communicate their needs. Under-
    standing that helps a person be more patient. Read
    this chapter carefully; read our coming book on
    Marriage and Parenting: A Guide for Religious Teens;
    and read other books on caring for children. Consider
    taking a class in family living or child care at your
    school. Ask your clergyperson to offer such a class
    at your church or synagogue.

*   We can be more patient when our lives are not too
    stressed in other ways. Having a decent income and
    a partner to help raise a child can make a difference.

*   We can be more patient when we feel good about
    ourselves. When we are upset with ourselves and
    impatient with ourselves, it's more difficult to be
    patient with anyone else–especially with an infant.

- We can be more patient when we *practice* being patient. When you start to feel angry with a child, take a moment to reflect on how much you love the child.

- We can be more patient when we pray for God's help and guidance. Praying helps us place God more at the center of our lives and opens us to the guidance that God wants to give us.

2. Good parents set a good example. Children learn both from what their parents say and what their parents do. When parents tell "white lies," children learn that it's okay to be dishonest some of the time. When parents treat one another or their children with disrespect, children learn that how they treat others doesn't matter. When parents smoke or drink, children are more likely to smoke or drink. When parents go to church or synagogue on a regular basis, children will grow up feeling that religious involvement is important. When parents donate to charity, children learn it's important to be generous.

Good parents recognize that almost everything they do has a positive or a negative impact on the lives of their children. They seek to be the kind of people they hope their children will become.

This doesn't mean that good parents are perfect. We are imperfect people living in an imperfect world, and all of us are going to make mistakes. The way that parents handle their own mistakes can help their children. Good parents acknowledge their mistakes, learn from their mistakes, and forgive themselves for their mistakes. A good parent who loses his or her temper and yells at a child apologizes for it. A good parent who locks the keys in the car takes the necessary steps to get in the car but doesn't make a big deal of it. Those kinds of things happen. Children need to know that mistakes are part of life and that there is no need to overreact.

3. Good parents are energetic. Parenting is fun work, but it is also hard work! Throw the ball a few more times, push the swing a few more times, run along behind the bike with the training wheel a couple more blocks. Cherish those moments even when they stretch your energy. [Remember that a time comes in the lives of most children when they don't even want to be seen with their parents!]

222

One of the major reasons that two parents find the parenting process easier than a single parent is that the workload can be shared. Parenting can be exhausting!

It's good to be physically fit before becoming a parent. Women who are healthy move through their pregnancies with fewer complications than persons who are seriously overweight, underweight, out-of-shape, or dealing with other health limitations. Both male and female parents continue to need energy as their children grow.

There are people who have health problems or physical challenges who are parents and who do a good job in spite of having lower energy than they would like. A partner, family members, and friends can all help. But you want to be as healthy as possible for the parenting years [and to make the most of your whole life].

4. Good parents help children develop a meaningful faith. While children have to develop their own religious faith, they are far more likely to do so with help from their parents. Parents need to talk comfortably about their beliefs and provide experiences that will help children develop their own faith. For example:

- Teach your children to pray before meals and at bedtime if you want prayer to be a meaningful part of their lives.

- Read Bible stories to your children as they grow. There are collections of Bible stories for children that use appropriate language and attractive illustrations to hold their interest.

- Involve your children in the life of a congregation through attendance at classes and other activities. Very few people choose to become involved in a congregation as adults if they did not have such experiences as children.

- Explain the ways that your faith affects your decisions. How does it affect the way you treat other people? How does it affect the way you spend money?

- Raise religious questions with your children when appropriate. When they are struggling with a decision, ask them what they think God would want them to do.

5. Good parents are empathetic. Find out and care about what's important to a child at a particular age, even if it seems like a trivial matter from an adult perspective. When a toddler has a blanket that he or she doesn't want to be without, remember that this is a serious matter for the toddler. When a second grader doesn't want to go to school because a playground bully has made life hard, recognize that this is a significant problem for the child. When a teenager feels crushed because he or she can't get a date for the prom, that is a very serious matter at the time.

The best parents think back to the experiences of their own childhood and remember how difficult some of them were. Most of us don't remember what it was like to be a toddler, but we remember some of our own elementary, middle school, and high school experiences. Being in touch with the joys and the sorrows of our own lives makes it easier for us to empathize with our children.

6. A good parent is unselfish. Don't neglect yourself, but put the child's needs ahead of your own. This is absolutely vital in the first months of life. Infants are totally dependent on adults. When they are hungry, they need to be fed. When their diapers are wet, the diapers need to be changed. When they have gas, they need to be burped. When they are unhappy, they need to be held. A parent may desperately want to be doing something else–watching television, reading a book, cleaning the kitchen, or perhaps, most desperately, sleeping! But the infant's needs must come first. While children don't demand the same kind of immediate attention as they grow older, the entire process of parenting brings many occasions when the needs of the child need to be put above the needs of the parent.

7. A good parent is involved. A good parent knows what is going on in his or her child's life. You don't have to be the soccer coach, the Brownie leader, the field trip chaperone, or the bus driver all of the time, but be one some of the time, as appropriate for your own skills.

When children participate in school plays, music or dance recitals, athletic events, and other activities, they feel rewarded when their parents attend and give them encouragement. Children can be disillusioned if their parents rarely attend their activities and can be even more disillusioned if parents say they will come and then fail to do so.

If you have two or three or four children, it won't be possible for you to be involved in all the events of all the children all the time. You want, however, to do as much as is realistically possible, and you want to give encouragement and show interest even when unable to attend.

If you've never played soccer, you probably aren't going to be the soccer coach; but you can still help by driving kids to practices and games and by offering other kinds of encouragement. If you've never been in a play or directed a play, it may be that the position of volunteer director of the school, church, or synagogue play isn't the position for you! But you can probably help by selling tickets or making costumes or doing publicity. Find the ways to help that are a good fit for you.

And be willing to stretch yourself sometimes. I was never involved in scouting myself as I grew up, but I had a lot of involvement with scouting when I had foster children who were scouts and when children in churches I pastored asked for my help with troop activities.

8. A good parent disciplines with love and consistency. Children need consistent guidelines and boundaries. Infants do not understand the consequences of their actions and should never be punished. As children grow, however, they do need clear expectations on how they behave, and there should be consequences when they disobey.

Physical punishment sends the message that hitting a loved one is okay. Other kinds of consequences are better, and consequences closely related to the negative behavior are best. For example:

- If your child is rude to another child or to an adult, require the child to offer a face-to-face apology for the rudeness.

- If your child refuses to get out of bed in time to get ready for school, don't write a note to excuse the behavior. Let your son or daughter live with the consequences.

- If a teenager drives recklessly, take away driving privileges for a period of time. [Hopefully this has never happened to you!]

- If a child isn't getting homework completed on time, take away television privileges on school nights until there's improvement.

The very best strategies are ones which prevent problems from happening. Talk with your children about the reasons for rules and expectations, and answer their questions. Always seek to understand the reasons for their failure to observe a boundary or an expectation. Listen to them as you want your own parents to listen to you! And explain things to them as you want your own parents to explain things to you.

9. A good parent has a sense of humor. The sooner you find that sense of humor when you're being peed on, washing yogurt out of a baby's hair, and re-rolling the unrolled toilet paper that's covering the bathroom floor, the easier things are.

Being a parent should be fun. The things that an infant does to make life difficult are not intentional. A sense of humor makes everything smoother, lowers blood pressure, and models a good attitude to children.

10. A good parent controls his or her anger. Know when to leave the room and how to control yourself. Apologize when appropriate.

Many people carry a heavy load of frustration. Teachers may be unfair; employers may be unfair; other drivers may be unfair; and clerks in stores may be unhelpful. It's easy to become angry, and it's often unwise to express that anger directly to the person responsible. The problem is that many people take their anger out on their spouses and children. A parent who gets chewed out by his or her supervisor at work may end up taking it out on a son or daughter. That isn't fair, even though it's a very common human behavior.

And children themselves can give plenty of reasons to make even the most patient and reasonable parent angry some of the time. The anger, however, almost never results in good communication or good decisions. Don't make decisions concerning your children [or much of anything else] when angry, and recognize that the best communication isn't going to happen when you are upset. Delay conversations until a calmer time if at all possible.

There are a few persons for whom anger is a persistent problem and who find themselves angry a great deal of the time. If that is the case for you, then you may need to consider getting professional help with anger management.

11. A good parent is available and honest. From whom would you want your child to get information about alcohol, drugs, tobacco, and sex? Start early in life providing real answers to all questions. Give as full an explanation as possible rather than short answers that leave important questions unanswered.

Very few parents feel like experts on topics like drugs and sex, but most parents know that they need to convey their values to their children. It's also possible to increase your knowledge through reading books, searching on the Internet, and attending classes. If you have a son or daughter ask a question for which you don't have an answer, work with them to find the answer.

Children don't necessarily raise important questions at the most convenient times. You may get asked a question about drugs or sex during a television show, at supper, or on the way to the grocery store. Whenever the question is asked, do your best to deal with it. If it really isn't possible to do so at that time, then make a commitment to have the conversation in the near future and honor that commitment.

12. A good parent wants to work himself or herself out of the parenting job but recognizes the relationship continues for life. My mother taught classes in Family Living for thirty years to high school students and to young adults. One of her consistent observations was this:

Many parents make the mistake of not controlling the behavior of their children when their children are young and the behavior is easily regulated. Then they find that their children are out of control in junior high or high school and start working to regain control. That very rarely works. The junior high and high school years are a period of time in which young people should become more self-regulating and self-directing. Trying to increase the amount of control during those years almost always has bad results. It's far better to have firm standards of behavior when children are young and help them become more self-regulating as they grow older. Once out of high school, they will need to be making almost all of their own decisions.

The best parents work themselves out of the parenting job as their children grow older. That avoids conflicts as their children are working to establish their own identity. That doesn't mean that parents should not have expectations on sons or daughters in high school, but the amount of parental control over a high school junior or senior should be much lower than over a first- or second-grade child.

The relationship between parents and children, however, continues throughout life. Love and the desire to spend time with one another should continue. Over the years, in healthy parent-child relationships, parents find themselves seeking guidance from their children as well as offering guidance to them.

Thinking about Your Own Parents and Being a Parent

Reading this chapter has no doubt caused you to think about your own parents and about how you have been raised. There is a natural tendency for us to base much of our own parenting style on the way that we have been raised ourselves. Where we feel that our parents have done a good job, we want to model our own parenting after their example. Where we feel that they have perhaps not done as good a job as was possible, we may take a different approach with our own children.

If you have a good relationship with your own parents, they can be a valuable resource as you think about the kind of parent you want to become. Even if you don't have a good relationship with them, you can probably still learn from them!

Being a good parent is an important job and sometimes a tough job! As you think more about what it means to be a good parent, you may find yourself feeling more understanding of the difficult decisions your own parents have had to make.

Through the gift of sexuality, God makes us part of the creative process. There is no more important life role than being a parent. When the time is right, may your own parenting experiences be filled with joy and meaning!

Chapter Fifteen
Where to Go for Help

*There are so many things I need to know and have
questions about. Where can you go for honest answers
and good information?*

Male–Assemblies of God

The Internet

I shared early in this book the caution that information on
health and sexuality through the Internet may not always be
reliable, especially when it comes from sexually explicit sites
that are designed to entertain rather than to inform. There are,
however, some sites on the Internet that provide information
which may be helpful to you. Please keep in mind that Internet
addresses change and that the management of Internet sites
can also change. This information is accurate as the book goes
to press:

Sex, ETC.: www.sxetc.org
This excellent site provides advice for teens about sexuality in a
FAQ [Frequently Asked Question] and story format. Major
topics include contraception, STDs, and sexual decision-making
with additional web links for each subject. The site also covers
topics like health, love and relationships, teen parenting,
abortion and adoption, abuse and violence, drugs, and body
image. This is a project of the "Network for Family Life
Education" by Rutgers University, so you can have confidence in
the accuracy of the information provided.

Teenwire: www.teenwire.com
This is also an excellent site and is managed by Planned
Parenthood. It's hip with cool graphics and teen language.
Topics include contraception, adoption, abortion, relationships,
pregnancy, emotional and sexual issues, world views, STDs, gay
issues, and more. There are also a lot of stories and topics
aimed at African and Hispanic audiences. You can count on
Planned Parenthood to offer current and accurate information
on sexuality.

Coalition for Positive Sexuality: www.positive.org
This is a down-to-earth site that provides a lot of information using teen language and illustrations. It's one of the most extensive and popular on the Internet.

Cool Nurse: www.coolnurse.com
This helpful site has information on various health-related concerns including topics like STDs, pregnancy, sexual FAQs [Frequently Asked Questions], contraception, and gynecology.

Teensexuality Information Center: www.teensexuality.com
This site offers general information on sexuality issues with an extensive page of links to other sites. Topics covered include understanding your sexuality, contraception, STDs, sexual health, and sexual assault. It is aimed at an older teen crowd or college students, and the link page is very good.

I wanna know: www.iwannaknow.org
This site is managed by the American Social Health Association. It offers sexual health and STD prevention information for teens including chat, education, games, and other resources. This site is very informative and has a section for parents too.

Puberty 101: www.puberty101.com
This is a great site for puberty issues including topics such as circumcision, penis size, wet dreams, sexual feelings, love, and underarm hair. The site also covers STDs, mental health, and drugs.

Campaign For Our Children Inc.: www.cfoc.org/teenguide
This site has a pro-life and an abstinence slant. The site includes an educator resource center and media/press area. Topics include abstinence, contraceptives, sexuality, date rape, STDs, and sexual abuse.

Scarleteen: www.scarleteen.com
This site is aimed at teenage girls and has a magazine feel to the layout and presentation. It promotes itself as delivering contemporary teen sex education and is a pro-choice site. Topics include sexuality, infection, reproduction, health, relationships, gay issues, and a crisis hotline. There is a section for parents.

gURL: www.gurl.com
This is another site aimed toward teen girls with a contemporary magazine feel. It covers topics such as being yourself, beliefs,

body image, dating, health, emotions, gynecology, birth control, date rape, petting, and abortion. It includes lots of polls and resources.

Boys Under Attack: www.boysunderattack.com
This is a fairly conservative Christian site. Topics include puberty, erections, gay issues, lust, pornography, and virginity. The site also covers God's love, terrorism and has an adult section.

Sistahs: www.mysistahs.org
This is a very interesting site especially aimed at adolescents of color and heavy on disease prevention. Health topics are covered as well as poetry and essays.

PFLAG: www.critpath.org/pflag-talk/
This is a large site dedicated to various gay issues concerning education, support, and advocacy. The site offers links, resources, a talk/chat line, and more. This is managed by the PFLAG [Parents, Family, and Friends of Lesbians and Gays] organization.

Youth.Org: www.youth.org
This is a site for gay and lesbian teens and offers emotional support and advice including links, a book list, toll free hotlines, and a directory of gay organizations.

Girl.mom: www.girlmom.com
This is a site for the support of teenage mothers and is supported by the Coalition for the Empowerment of Teen Parents. The site is written by teens for teens and includes lots of stores, articles, and essays.

Telephone Numbers

Some of the websites listed above also offer toll-free numbers. In this section I want to briefly highlight some additional telephone numbers that could be valuable to you.

Backline: 1-888-493-0092. Backline offers a toll free, confidential talk line for women and their loved ones to explore pregnancy, abortion, adoption, and parenting. Callers from all over the United States can speak to an Advocate about the wide range of feelings and questions they may have and receive

231

support, resources, and tools for communication and decision-making. The telephone number is the most important resource, but they also have a website at www.yourbackline.org

Other numbers:

National Eating Disorders Association: 1-800-931-2237

National Drug and Alcohol Treatment Hotline 1-800-662-HELP

National Domestic Violence Hotline 1-800-799-7233

National Child Abuse Hotline 1-800-4-A-CHILD

National Youth Crisis Hotline 1-800-HIT-HOME

National Adolescent Suicide Hotline 1-800-621-4000

The Teen AIDS Hotline 1-800-440-TEEN

National AIDS Hot Line at (800) 342-AIDS

Organizations

Planned Parenthood. There are Planned Parenthood affiliates all over the United States. Many people associate Planned Parenthood so strongly with the abortion debate that they fail to recognize Planned Parenthood's extensive involvement in sexuality education with the provision of accurate information to people of all ages. You can look up the local office in your phone book or call 1-800-230-7526. Planned Parenthood Federation of America, 434 West 33rd St. New York, NY 10001. www.plannedparenthood.org

Christian Community. That's the organization responsible for the book that you hold in your hands. Christian Community focuses on research and resource development to benefit congregations and the communities in which they minister. In addition to research and development on teens and sexuality, the organization has also developed resources on faith-sharing, hospitality, worship, and stewardship. **Teens with questions can contact Steve Clapp here.** 6404 S. Calhoun Street, Fort Wayne, Indiana 46807. 800-774-3360. DadofTia@aol.com; www.churchstuff.com

The other organizations listed here are somewhat more for adults who are looking at this book and want resources:

The Center for the Prevention of Sexual and Domestic Violence. This organization works with faith-based institutions to address sexual and domestic violence. They offer books, videos, and seminars. They can refer victims to sources of counseling in a local area. 2400 N. 45th Street, Suite 10, Seattle, Washington 98103. 206-634-1903. www.cpsdv.org

The Black Church Initiative. This is a project of the Religious Coalition for Reproductive Choice and has the goal of breaking the silence about sexuality in African-American churches. They have sexuality education curricula for both adults and teens, and they hold an annual National Black Religious Summit on Sexuality. 1025 Vermont Avenue, N.W., Suite 1130, Washington, DC. www.rcrc.org

The Religious Institute for Sexual Morality, Justice, and Healing. This is an ecumenical, interfaith organization dedicated to advocating for sexual health, education, and justice in faith communities and society. They offer resources, consulting, and seminars to help congregations become sexually healthy faith communities. 304 Main Avenue, #335, Norwalk, Connecticut 06851. 203-840-1148. www.religiousinstitute.org

National Campaign to Prevent Teen Pregnancy. This organization brings together people from many different fields in cooperative efforts to prevent teen pregnancy. They offer a wide range of resources, including some developed especially for religious institutions. They have a website packed with helpful information including materials you can download without charge. 1776 Massachusetts Avenue, N.W., #200, Washington, DC 20036. 202-478-8518. www.teenpregnancy.org

SIECUS: Sexuality Information and Education Council of the United States. This organization offers a large number of resources in the area of sexuality education and has helped set standards for sexuality education that have influenced many people and organizations, including the author of this book. Suite 350, 130 West 42nd Street, New York, New York 10036. 212-819-9770. www.siecus.org

The Center for Sexuality and Religion. This organization focuses on the education of clergy in the area of sexuality and works in cooperation with seminaries. 987 Old Eagle School Road, Suite 719, Wayne, Pennsylvania 19087-1708. 610-995-0341. www.CTRSR.org

Our Whole Lives. This is a comprehensive sexuality education curriculum designed for use in faith-based institutions. It was developed by the Unitarian Universalist Association and the United Church of Christ and is the most complete and accurate curriculum available for religious communities. *Our Whole Lives* is a series of sexuality education curricula for five age groups: grades K-1, grades 4-6, grades 7-9, grades 10-12, and adults. *Our Whole Lives* helps participants make informed and responsible decisions about their sexual health and behavior. It equips participants with accurate, age-appropriate information in six subject areas: human development, relationships, personal skills, sexual behavior, sexual health, and society and culture. Grounded in a holistic view of sexuality, *Our Whole Lives* provides not only facts about anatomy and human development, but helps participants to clarify their values, build interpersonal skills, and understand the spiritual, emotional, and social aspects of sexuality. This is excellent material for churches. www.uua.org/owl/what.html or www.ucc.org/justice/owl

Group Publishing. This is a nondenominational organization that provides a variety of resources for Christian congregations including some which deal with sexuality. You'll find many helpful materials here. P.O. Box 481, Loveland, Colorado 80539. 1-800-447-1070. www.grouppublishing.com

Youth Specialties. This is another nondenominational organization offering a variety of resources for youth work including some that deal with sexuality. 300 S. Pierce Street, El Cajon, California 92029. 1-619-440-2333. www.youthspecialties.com

Your own denomination likely offers resources to help youth in the area of sexuality; space doesn't permit a full listing here. You'll find more about denominational contacts and books of interest in the *Adult Guide* that is available to accompany this book.

Appendix
The Faith Matters Study

My priest, the church, my parents would consider me
a slut if they knew what I did. . . . I don't think I'm
that different than any other teenager. I can't wait to
see the results of this. Like I take my religion seriously,
but I can't agree with NO birth control, NO premarital
sex, NO abortion under any circumstances.

Female–Roman Catholic Church

Most authors want people to read every single word that they write. I don't feel that way. That's why this section appears as an Appendix rather than as a main chapter in the book. Much of the content of this book is based on the *Faith Matters* study that I directed on how the religious faith and involvement of teenagers relates to their sexual values and behaviors. Or to put it another way: how does congregational activity relate to sexual activity? This section tells you some of the background of that study.

If you are primarily interested in the information about sexuality and faith in this book and don't care much about surveys and procedures, this material may not be interesting to you. But if you are curious about how the study was conducted and who took part in it, then this chapter will answer some of your questions.

Who Completed Surveys?

Surveys were returned by 5,819 youth in grades nine through twelve from 635 congregations. Slightly more females (3,070) than males (2,739) completed surveys, which is consistent with the fact that most Protestant and Catholic congregations in the United States have slightly more female teenagers than male teenagers involved.

4,198 of the surveys were completed by Protestant youth who came from 38 different denominations. Surveys were also completed by 819 Roman Catholic youth. The 361 Jewish youth completing surveys came from both Reform and

Conservative congregations, but none was from an Orthodox Jewish congregation.

Surveys were returned by 207 Islamic youth. There were surveys from 103 youth whom we classified as "other" in terms of religious affiliation; those included youth in the Buddhist and Hindu traditions as well as some youth who are in what might be called "new age" faith communities.

Respondents by Religious Affiliation

4,198	Protestant
819	Roman Catholic
131	Unitarian
361	Jewish
207	Islamic
103	Other

Some readers will be interested in the denominations included under the broad category of "Protestant." They are listed here in order of youth surveys received beginning with the United Methodist Church, from which we received the most surveys, and ending with the Primitive Baptist Church, from which we received the smallest number of surveys:

United Methodist Church	Church of the Brethren
Presbyterian Church, USA	Mennonite Church
Southern Baptist Churches	Pentecostal Holiness Church
Missouri Synod Lutheran	Reformed Church in America
Evangelical Lutheran Church	Free Methodist Church
African Methodist Episcopal	Progressive Baptist Church
United Church of Christ	Church of Jesus Christ of
Disciples of Christ	Latter Day Saints
American Baptist Churches	Evangelical Covenant Church
African Methodist Episcopal Zion	Friends
Episcopal Church	United Pentecostal Church
Assemblies of God	National Primitive Baptist
Church of God	Moravian Church
Nazarene Church	Brethren Church
Black Baptist Church	Brethren in Christ Church
Christian Methodist Episcopal	Independent Baptist Church
Missionary Church	Missionary Alliance Church
Independent Christian Churches	Wesleyan Church
Pentecostal Church	Primitive Baptist Church
Cumberland Presbyterian Church	

If you are a member of the Brethren Church, the Church of the Brethren, the Mennonite Church, or the Brethren in Christ, you may be aware that these denominations think of themselves as Anabaptist rather than Protestant. For the purposes of this study, however, we grouped them together because of the similarities in belief.

Two-thirds of the youth who completed surveys are white, but the other third includes African American, Hispanic/Latino, Native American, and Asian youth. Every state was represented except New Hampshire and Utah. We had nothing against New Hampshire and Utah and tried to get participation from congregations in those states, but it just didn't happen.

A few Canadian churches learned of the study and asked to participate in the survey process. While we were pleased to share the surveys with those congregations, the results were not included both because the focus was on the United States and because all the United States congregations were ones whose participation we requested based on a carefully developed sampling process rather than ones which approached us.

The teens came from a broad range of household incomes and every conceivable living arrangement including traditional husband-and-wife households, single parent homes, non-married couple households, foster homes, and households headed by couples of the same sex. Some lived with their grandparents or in the home of a friend rather than with their own parents, and some were living in children's homes or other institutional settings. A few were married, and a few were parents.

Congregational Involvement

The youth in this study are all active in their churches or synagogues. Not all of them attend worship services every single week, but their overall frequency of attendance is high. Over 80% of teens in this study attended religious services at least two or three times a month.

Attendance at Religious Services

53.8%	Attend religious services one or more times a week
26.9%	Attend religious services two or three times a month
9.5%	Attend religious services once a month
7.1%	Attend religious services less than once a month
2.7%	Never attend religious services

Activity in a youth group, youth class, choir, or other congregational program was higher than attendance at religious services for the youth in this study. Over 90% participate in a youth group, class, choir, or other congregational program at least two or three times a month. Those youth in our study who do not attend religious services were nevertheless active in other aspects of congregational life–especially in a youth class or group.

Some small congregations are not able to offer activities just for youth, but many youth in those congregations still participate in a class with adults or with younger children. Some large congregations offer an enormous range of activities for youth including sports groups, drama groups, Bible study groups, prayer groups, personal growth groups, film-making groups, and a variety of musical groups. There are youth who attend weekly Bible study groups that meet at six o'clock in the morning!

Sixty-two percent of the youth had been involved in some kind of service project through their faith-based institution. Those projects ranged from doing yard clean-up for elderly members of the congregation to traveling to other countries to help build or renovate housing for the poor. Sixteen percent of the youth in this study have helped build a Habitat for Humanity home in the United States, working with others in their congregation.

Faith is very important in the lives of almost all of these teens. Most of the teens say that they pray daily or at least weekly (95.3%), and most feel that their faith does relate to the decisions they make in their daily lives (90.2%). We asked the teens about the importance of faith in their lives: 70.5% said faith is very important in their lives, and 23.3% said it is fairly important

Comments about Taking the Survey

Here are a few comments from teens about the process of taking the survey and about the link between their faith and their sexuality:

> *I was like in shock when this survey was given to the youth group. We NEVER talk about any of this. People totally think this doesn't belong in the church. But we'll have some interesting talk after we've sealed these in the envelopes.* Male–Southern Baptist Church

> *My minister and youth advisor encourage us to talk about sex. That's helped me sort out what I believe and how I want to live. . . But this survey makes me realize there are some topics we haven't covered yet.* Female–United Church of Christ

> *I'm sure glad we seal these in envelopes and put them in the mail rather than handing them in. I could never have been honest if there was any chance that my teacher or pastor would find out what I had done or what I thought.* Male–Church of God

> *This is the one topic we never touch. The only thing the church wants to say about sex is DON'T DO IT. But that isn't enough. Filling this out makes me think there must be some churches that are doing more. Are there?* Female–Evangelical Lutheran Church

As you can tell from the comments, we provided an individual envelope to each person who took the survey. That let people seal their completed surveys in the envelopes and mail them directly back to us. We didn't want there to be any chance that their minister or youth leader would look at their survey responses.

The other people who conducted the study and I also met with teenagers individually and in groups all around the United

States. Their sharing helped us better understand the written comments on the surveys.

Some people who are reading this book may have completed a survey for us or may have participated in an interview or a group discussion. Thank you! The really honest comments of so many teenagers are what provided much of the information that I am sharing with you in this book.

To order:
- More copies of this book.
- The *Adult Guide* which is a companion to this book.
- *Faith Matters*, which gives the full results of the study on which *The Gift of Sexuality* is based.
- The coming book *Marriage and Parenting: A Guide for Religious Teens.*
- Other resources on youth, religion, and sexuality.

Call:

Christian Community/LifeQuest
800-774-3360

Or ask your bookseller to call for you.